USAF INTERCEPTORS

A MILITARY PHOTO LOGBOOK (1946–1979)

Compiled by Marty J. Isham & David R. McLaren

specialtypress
PUBLISHERS AND WHOLESALERS

Specialty press

PUBLISHERS AND WHOLESALERS

Specialty Press
39966 Grand Avenue
North Branch, MN 55056
Phone: 651-277-1400 or 800-895-4585
Fax: 651-277-1203
www.specialtypress.com

Edit by Mike Machat
Layout by Monica Seiberlich

ISBN 978-1-58007-150-5
Item No. SP150

Library of Congress Cataloging-in-Publication Data

Isham, Marty J.
   USAF interceptors : a military photo logbook, 1946-1979 / by Marty J. Isham and David R. McLaren.
      p. cm.
   ISBN 978-1-58007-150-5
   1. Fighter planes–United States–History–Pictorial works. 2. Jet planes, Military–United States–History–Pictorial works. 3. Airplanes, Military–United States–History–Pictorial works. 4. United States. Air Force. Air Defense Command–History–Pictorial works. I. McLaren, David R. II. Title.
   UG1242.F5I82 2010
   623.74'64097309045–dc22
                                          2010001229

Printed in China
10 9 8 7 6 5 4 3 2 1

Front Cover:
A Convair F-102A Delta Dagger conducts a live salvo firing of Hughes GAR-1 Falcon radar-guided air-to-air missiles from within its three internal weapons bays over the Yuma Proving Ground on 25 August 1958. The Dagger was the first operational U.S. fighter to carry missiles internally rather than on underwing pylons. (Convair, courtesy of the Bill Yenne Collection)

Table of Contents Page:
With its missile tray lowered and ready to receive a full load of 24 "Mighty Mouse" rockets, a North American F-86L poses on the ramp at Charleston AFB, South Carolina, in summer 1957. Flown by the 444th Fighter Interceptor Squadron, this radar-nose Sabre represented an earlier generation of jet interceptor and was replaced by the supersonic twin-engine McDonnell F-101B Voodoo. (U.S. Air Force)

Back Cover (Top):
Lockheed's sleek F-104 Starfighter was the world's first operational Mach 2 aircraft, and was considered well ahead of its time when it first flew in 1954. Designed right from the start as a manned high-performance Air Defense interceptor, the F-104 served with the air arms of numerous foreign nations, some of which used the jet for more than four decades. (U.S. Air Force)

Back Cover (Bottom):
The Squadron Commander's airplane usually wore special markings, and this Mach 2 Convair F-106A Delta Dart was certainly no exception. This photo shows the Dart flown by the Commander of the 5th Fighter Interceptor Squadron based at Minot AFB, North Dakota. The unit was also known as the famed "Spittin' Kittens." (Frank MacSorley)

Distributed in the UK and Europe by
Crécy Publishing Ltd
1a Ringway Trading Estate
Shadowmoss Road
Manchester M22 5LH England
Tel: 44 161 499 0024
Fax : 44 161 499 0298
www.crecy.co.uk
enquiries@crecy.co.uk

Contents

Preface

This photo logbook is not a definitive study, but rather a short insight into the interceptors used by the Air Defense Command from 1946 to 1979. While space won't allow us to cover every aircraft used by every ADC Fighter Interceptor Squadron, we do hope you enjoy these photographs as you go back to those thrilling days of yesteryear. With this photo research, Dave and I have been able to further and keep alive an important part of the history of the United States Air Force, the Air Defense Command.

Marty J. Isham
David R. McLaren

Dedication

To all the members of the Air Defense Command,
from beginning to end,
on the ground and in the air!

Acknowledgments

We wish to thank the following friends and contributors who have assisted us through the years with slides, photographs, and the histories used in this photo logbook: W. J. Balough, Sr., J. Balzer, D. Barbier, R. Besecker, G. Bracken, T. Brewer, B. Butcher, T. Chong, T. Cuddy, B. Curry, L. Davis, B. Dorr, M. Druzolowski, B. Esposito, R. Francillon, P. Friddell, H. Gann, J. Geer, B. Green, B. Greenhalgh, R. Harrison, J. Kolln, T. Landis, W. Larkins, R. Lawson, B. Livesay, D. Logan, F. MacSorley, R. McCarthy, D. Menard, S. Miller, J. Morris, D. Olson, D. Ostrowski, L. Paul, R. Picciani, B. Rys, R. Sherry, D. Slowiak, P. Stevens, B. Strandberg, N. Taylor, W. Thompson, J. Wogstad, D. Wood, and B. Yokum.

Special thanks to Erv Smalley and Don Logan for their terrific support with all the computer wizardry that makes possible a modern book such as this one.

If we've forgotten anyone, we really didn't mean to do so. Thanks again to all!

Chapter One

A 5th FS P-61B, 42-39567, awaits its next flight in 1948. PK-567 was delivered from the Tinker AFB depot on 21 December 1947. (Isham Collection)

The Formative Years

P-47 Thunderbolt, P-51 Mustang, P-61 Black Widow, F-82 Twin Mustang

When we hear the words "fighter interceptor," images of shiny supersonic jets usually come to mind. However, in the first days of the Air Defense Command's existence, piston-powered aircraft left over from World War II comprised all of the fighter assets the Army Air Forces (and later U.S. Air Force) had available.

The Beginnings

World War II taught leaders of the Army Air Forces (AAF) that the primary missions of an air force were strategic and tactical aerial operations and air defense. The Battle of Britain served as a paramount example of the need for and results of good air defense. In the spring of 1946, the remnants of our great World War II air armada were reorganized for peacetime duty, and the AAF reasoned that this peacetime structure should allow continued development for these three basic missions.

In keeping with this logic for national air defense, the Air Defense Command (ADC) was created and activated on 27 March 1946, with headquarters at Mitchel Field, New York. In command of ADC was Lt. General George B. Stratemeyer. ADC assumed command of the 414th Night Fighter Squadron, which was purely an organization on paper at the time, as well as the 425th Night Fighter Squadron, with only three people assigned. Two bases, Mitchel Field on Long Island and Hamilton Field in California, were also assigned to ADC. Because these were relatively smaller and much older bases, this was a rather poor beginning for the Command's fighter forces. As a further organization in the chain of command, ADC Fighter Interceptor Squadron (FIS) forces would come under control of numbered Air Forces.

The mission assigned to ADC was to organize and operate the intricate network of military assets that would ensure the integrated air defense of the continental United States. However, it became immediately clear that the Command's ability to carry out this mission was severely limited. Most of the combat forces left to the AAF in this timespan went to the creation of the heavy bomber forces' Strategic Air Command (SAC). Also, U.S. Army demands for combat air support required that Tactical Air Command (TAC) forces be given the next highest priority in aircraft and men. What was left went to ADC.

By 10 June 1946, the ADC mission was expanded so that the Command was required to coordinate within the means available from other services, namely the U.S. Navy and U.S. Marine Corps, for air defense. These Navy and Marine aircraft, when temporarily shore-based, would be vital to ADC. At this time, the command charged with defending the nation against air attack was so weak, that at best, it could only act as a sort of "clearing house" of aerial assets for the future air defense of the United States. General Stratemeyer and his staff were not able to speak with a firm voice at this time, as they were helpless to get increased funding beyond Army levels.

Finally, on 18 September 1947, the United States Air Force (USAF) was created as a separate branch of the U.S. armed forces. As such, USAF and ADC were granted their independence and now achieved equal status with the Army and Navy.

On 17 December, USAF heeded ADC warnings and granted ADC the authority to use fighter and radar forces of SAC, TAC, and the Air National Guard (ANG) in an emergency. The major source of the air defense units were to come from the ANG force. For the first time since the end of the war, the Air Force was in a position to finally "put some teeth" into an air defense program. At this point, however, the Russians decided to heat up the Cold War by effectively blockading East Berlin. General Lucias Clay in Berlin reported on 5 March 1948 that the Russians were ready to start World War III. In response, USAF ordered ADC to provide air defense to the northwestern United States to protect the Hanford atomic works, and the New York–Washington, D.C., corridor on the East Coast.

By the time the "crisis" had blown over in mid-April, only a semblance of an air defense system had been put together. The mounting Cold War tensions finally convinced Congress of the need for some serious air defense activity. All U.S. services gave their reasoning as to why they should be the one to ultimately control air defense. The new secretary of defense, James V. Forrestal, on 21 April 1948, finally gave his decision: The newly established Air Force would have the primary responsibility for air defense of the United States. Now General Stratemeyer and his staff could begin to implement their long-awaited plans.

On 25 October 1948, ADC's future came into clearer focus. The first air division for defense, the 25th Air Division, was established at Silver Lake, Washington (near Everett). Air defense had finally come to the West Coast. The 26th Air Division was formed on the East Coast, at Roslyn, Long Island, New York, on 16 November. With the Cold War gaining in intensity and scope with each passing month, USAF and ADC planners finally realized that the meager resources of the current Air Defense Command were not enough, especially when it came to the actual aircraft.

Fighter strength was increased on 1 December 1948 by pooling the missions and forces of ADC and TAC under a new organization called the Continental Air Command (ConAC), with headquarters at Mitchel AFB. SAC also gave up three fighter wings with nine squadrons to ConAC. Overall responsibility for air defense was now in the hands of ConAC. With this reorganization ADC and TAC became operational headquarters, with no operational units assigned. ADC became just a small staff of planners. This reorganization finally brought air defense to equal or greater importance than tactical air. Experts predicted that if Russia were to attack the U.S. in late-1948, air defense needs would have to be considered over tactical air (if the Air Force had to choose between the two).

In 1949 a pattern of air defense organization began to take shape. In March, the 25th and 26th Air Divisions assumed air defense responsibilities from the Fourth and First Air Forces respectively. On 1 July, Headquarters ADC was discontinued as an unnecessary echelon between ConAC Headquarters and air defense forces. On 1 September, the Eastern and Western Air Defense Forces were activated at Mitchel AFB, and Hamilton AFB, California, respectively, and new air divisions were activated as well. These divisions would command sectors. At the end of 1949, responsibility for the air defense of the nation rested solely with the commander of ConAC and was carried out on a regional and sector basis through the Air Defense Forces and Air Division commanders.

In August 1949, just after these changes were implemented, Russia detonated its first atomic device years earlier than what U.S. experts predicted. Seemingly overnight, USAF and ConAC found themselves with serious and major shortcomings in their air defense plans and programs. More funds were suddenly granted by Congress for greater expansion of air defense, which led to a better plan in the deployment of the fighter forces of ConAC. Prior to this, the three squadrons of each wing were located on the same base as the wing headquarters. Under the new plan, the squadrons were now deployed to different individual air force bases. Alert facilities could now be found on both TAC and SAC bases, and this gave ConAC's fighter forces greater dispersal in case of a surprise attack.

On 25 June 1950 war broke out in Korea. Any remaining doubts in Congress and the Department of Defense (DOD) as to the need for strong air defense of the United States disappeared. Increased manning began throughout the air defense forces with the call-up of Air Force Air National Guard and Reserve personnel. The Cold War was becoming hotter. This increase in manning caused two important changes to the air defense organization. On 1 July 1950, ADC was discontinued and ConAC controlled all the air defense forces in the United States. By August 1950, the Air Defense Forces headquarters were fully manned after having taken over full command of the tactical forces from the numbered air forces. In November, plans were laid for making air defense the sole responsibility of a single major Air Force command. This allowed the air defense commander to give his full attention to air defense. The change was long overdue since, beginning in 1946, the air defense commander had been responsible for several major duties, with the result being that air defenses never got the full attention they deserved.

Keeping in mind the old, but wise, saying, "history repeats itself," on 1 January 1951, ADC was reconstituted and reestablished as a major air command at Mitchel AFB. Only one week later, ADC headquarters moved to Ent AFB in Colorado Springs, Colorado. ADC inherited from ConAC a regular fighter force of only 21 squadrons. ConAC remained in existence at Mitchel AFB to supervise the air force reserves and related missions. At the same time TAC also resumed its former status as a major Air Force command.

New Beginnings and a Stronger Air Defense

The new command moved quickly ahead in improving air defense. On 1 February 1951, 18 ANG units were mobilized and assigned to ADC as Fighter Interceptor Squadrons. Three more ANG units were assigned on 1 March. This was further testimony of the DOD's anxiety to strengthen air defenses with the Korean War in progress. Also on 1 March, a new regional command was formed to take charge of the air defense forces in the mid-section of the nation. This was the Central Air Defense Force (CADF) with headquarters at Grandview AFB, Missouri. By July, the three Defense Force regions, Eastern, Central, and Western, had the air defense of the nation well in hand (at least on paper).

A reorganization of ADC on 8 February 1952 ended the wing-base plan and created actual air defense wings. On 1 November and 1 December 1952, 21 ANG squadrons were released from active duty. Each of these released squadrons were replaced by a newly activated regular FIS, and in some cases at a different base other than that occupied by the ANG squadron. These new FISs retained the same aircraft assigned to the ANG squadron.

Another reorganization of ADC took place on 16 February 1953 with the defense wings now assigned to air divisions. One of the most important reorganizations to ADC at this time had its beginnings in late 1950. This was the changeover from conventional and day jet aircraft to a jet all-weather interceptor force. The inability of the interceptor force to fly and fight through overcasts and under night and cold weather conditions had been one of the major weaknesses in the U.S. air defense system since 1946. The first all-weather jets to be assigned to ADC were the Lockheed F-94A and F-94B, modified versions of the venerable T-33A trainer. The first Northrop F-89s were assigned in June 1951. The F-86D, an all-weather version of North American's famed Sabre jet, began to arrive at ADC in April 1953. The advanced F-94C Starfire, an improved version of the original F-94, arrived at ADC in March 1953. By 30 June 1955, the FIS force was made up totally of new all-weather interceptors.

The rapid growth of fighter aircraft forces of all three services at this time led to another reorganization within ADC. This was the creation of the Continental Air Defense Command (CONAD) at Ent AFB on 1 September 1954. Established directly under the Joint Chiefs of Staff, with the Air Force (ADC) serving as the executive agency, the new organization was a tri-service command designed to weld together the full military resources of the nation.

This new command was unique in military history. Joint headquarters were formed alongside each ADC echelon through the air divisions. Keeping manning costs to a minimum, the staffs of the joint commands were formed by assigning ADC officers the dual role of fulfilling duties of their positions on both staffs. A small number of Army and Navy officers were then assigned to the joint headquarters as their sole responsibility. Additionally, separate Army and Navy organizations were established alongside the ADC headquarters at each echelon, wherever necessary. Commanders of these joint headquarters, along with the commanders of the Army and Navy components, served as principal advisors for their respective functions. The Air Defense Force commanders were appointed to the command of the Joint Air Defense Forces and the Air Division (Defense) commanders assumed command of the Joint

Air Defense Divisions. With the activation of CONAD, primary responsibility for the air defense of the nation passed from ADC to the new organization. History had repeated itself once again.

In August 1955, another reorganization of ADC took place. In three years the FIS force expanded rapidly with the activation of new FISs. Summer 1955 saw an ADC FIS Force of 58 squadrons with 1,404 aircraft. This new reorganization, known as Project Arrow, restored squadrons to Groups and Wings, the organizational structure with which they were associated during World War II. All moves now involved less personnel and equipment. In August 1955, the deactivation of the air defense groups and activation of "fighter groups (air defense)" in their place, coupled with the geographical realignment of squadrons, would reestablish the traditional chain of command between Air Force Squadrons and Groups.

The CONAD reorganization also brought about additions to the FIS alert forces. On 1 October 1955,

Project Arrow

The Project Arrow changes were as follows:

TRANSFERS

Squadron	Old Base	New Base
2	McGuire	Suffolk
5	McGuire	Suffolk
13	Selfridge	Sioux City
42	O'Hare	Greater Pittsburgh
56	Selfridge	Wright-Patterson
60	Westover	Otis
63	Wurtsmith	O'Hare
71	Greater Pittsburgh	Selfridge
75	Suffolk	Presque Isle
82	Presque Isle	Travis
83	Paine	Hamilton
94	George	Selfridge
97	Wright-Patterson	New Castle
318	Presque Isle	McChord
323	Larson	Truax
325	Hamilton	Truax
331	Suffolk	Stewart
332	New Castle	McGuire
337	Minneapolis-St Paul	Westover
354	Oxnard	McGhee-Tyson
432	Truax	Minneapolis-St. Paul
437	Otis	Oxnard
445	Geiger	Wurtsmith
456	Truax	Castle
460	McGhee-Tyson	Portland
465	McChord	Griffiss
497	Portland	Geiger
539	Stewart	McGuire

ACTIVATIONS

Squadron	Base
76	Presque Isle
321	Paine
322	Larson
327	George
329	George
498	Geiger
538	Larson

DEACTIVATIONS

Squadron	Base
31	Larson
413	Travis
518	George
519	Sioux City
520	Geiger

the Air Training Command began placing fighters on daily air defense alert at Perrin AFB, Texas, and on 1 December, the Navy also began a daily air defense alert at NAS North Island in San Diego, California. Even the Air Force Reserve, with the 319 Fighter Bomber Wing (FBW), began standing "dawn-to-dusk" five-minute alerts at Memphis, Tennessee, on 1 July 1956, using two Republic F-84E Thunderjets. The 319 FBW ended its ADC alert commitment on 1 August 1957.

With the advent of the Semi-Automatic Ground Environment (SAGE) System, a message was sent in August 1956 to all ADC wings operating a direction center notifying them that beginning in January 1957, they would be designated as an Air Defense Sector. The year 1957 saw the ADC at its absolute peak, and by 30 June, the Command had 71 squadrons assigned (although two were not equipped with personnel and aircraft) with an impressive total of 1,500 interceptors listed in the Air Force inventory.

Air Defense of the United States Begins Its Decline

After the 1957 "peak" of ADC interceptor forces, events began to occur that started the decline of FIS forces in ADC. In July 1956, the CIA began its Top Secret Lockheed U-2 reconnaissance overflights of the Soviet Union, and photos began to show that the Russian bomber threat against the United States was not what it was first thought to be by Air Force intelligence. Then, on 4 October 1957, the Russians launched Sputnik into orbit. This brought about Congressional arguments about a "missile gap" and a "technology decline," and that funds spent on bomber defense were excessive and wasted! So in June 1959, the DOD issued a Master Air Defense Plan which, in part, canceled plans to upgrade the aircraft of the ADC interceptor forces. As we now know, purchases of McDonnell F-101Bs and Convair F-106s were severely reduced. ADC leaders fought for upgraded and additional air defense assets throughout the 1960s and 1970s, but to no avail. Even though ADC proposed plans for a highly advanced new aircraft called the Improved Manned Interceptor (IMI), this new program was simply not forthcoming.

With the clear focus being placed on a massive "first strike" attack of Soviet Intercontinental Ballistic Missiles (ICBMs), the fact that a potent force of manned and nuclear-armed Bear bombers could still follow an ICBM attack seemed to go by the wayside. Theoretically, a minimum force of 150 to 200 bombers could still wreak havoc on U.S. population centers if they were employed on a one-way target run. To complicate matters further, the intensifying air war in Southeast Asia also cut into air defense plans and funding during the mid 1960s. Adding insult to injury, two Convair F-102 FISs, the 82nd and 64th, were transferred to the Pacific Air Forces (PACAF) for Southeast Asia service in June 1966.

By the late-1960s, ADC's principal FIS assets were the F-101 Voodoos and the F-106 Delta Darts. In the 1970s, however, FIS forces were reduced primarily to F-106s. The 57th FIS at Keflavik, Iceland, received its F-102s in July 1962 and then McDonnell F-4C Phantom IIs in April 1973. Gun-nose F-4Es arrived in March 1978.

With the space mission growing in ADC, the command changed its name to Aerospace Defense Command on 15 January 1968. In 1971 the F-101Bs left ADC for the Air National Guard and the F-106s began to leave for the ANG in April 1972. On 1 July 1975, ADC was designated a specified command by the Joint Chiefs of Staff and was called "ADCOM."

Then on 1 September 1975, General Daniel "Chappie" James, Jr., assumed command of ADCOM/NORAD. Chappie was certainly no stranger to the air defense arena; he commanded the 437th FIS at Otis AFB, Massachusetts, in 1953 when that unit became the first F-94C squadron in ADC. He wanted the Air Force to seriously consider upgrading its interceptor force with Grumman's new swing-wing F-14 Tomcat, but was later told in no uncertain terms that after procuring Douglas AD Skyraiders, McDonnell F-4 Phantom IIs, and Vought A-7 Corsair IIs, the Air Force was *not* going to buy another Navy airframe! Chappie James was replaced by General James E. Hill on 6 December 1978, and shortly thereafter, suffered a massive fatal heart attack.

Finally, in one last air defense reorganization to reduce supposed overhead in management, what dwindling ADCOM air defense forces were left were unceremoniously transferred to the TAC on 1 October 1979. Five FISs were transferred to TAC, still flying the 1950s-era F-106 Delta Dart: the 5th, 48th, 49th, 87th, and 318th. They would become the very last operational Air Force Squadrons to fly Convair's magnificent Mach 2 delta-wing fighter. The 57th FIS in Iceland with F-4Es also had the TAC patch applied to its aircrafts' tails. With this final reorganization, ADCOM didn't last very long and was officially deactivated at Colorado Springs, Colorado, on 31 March 1980. A proud and vital era in the history of the United States Air Force had finally come to an end.

As impressive as this airplane may have been at the end of World War II, in ADC the Northrop P-61B interceptor force was virtually useless. Even under ideal conditions, it was no match for bombers like the B-29 (or the Russian copy, the TU-4 Bull), as the P-61 only had a top speed of about 360 mph and a service ceiling of only 30,000 feet. When the 425 night fighter squadron (NFS) got its P-61s from depots, only 12 were assigned to the squadron. Of all the Air Defense Command squadrons, only four would fly the Black Widow, and records indicate that a total of only 46 P-61s were assigned to ADC from 1946 to 1949.

Note that after the Air Force became a separate branch of the Armed Forces on 18 September 1947, several changes were made to once sacrosanct designations. On 13 January 1948, all existing "Army Air Fields" became "Air Force Bases," while on 11 June 1948, all existing "Pursuit" aircraft (P-47, P-51, etc.) were changed to "Fighter" aircraft (F-47, F-51, etc.). All fighters manufactured after that date would be

This is one of ADC's first assigned P-61Bs, 43-8293, PK-293, to the 425th NFS at McChord Field from the Kansas Depot on 8 September 1946. (S. Staples)

P-61B-20, 43-8279 was assigned to the 318th FS at Hamilton on 15 December 1947. The airplane was struck from the inventory on 20 December 1948. (B. Esposito)

A 2nd FS P-61B, 42-39556, on the Mitchel AFB ramp, was delivered on 22 January 1948 from the Tinker AFB depot in Oklahoma. It went to Pope AFB, North Carolina, on 16 March 1948. (B. Esposito)

P-61Bs of the 2nd and 5th FSs of the 52nd FG sit on the Mitchel AFB ramp in February 1948. (USAF)

On the Mitchel AFB ramp is Genny, a 2nd FS (AW) P-61B, 43-8233, assigned on 23 October 1948 from the 318th. Flat Top (in the background) belonged to the CO of the 5th, a P-61B, 43-8290. (USAF)

Four P-61Bs of the 2nd Fighter Squadron (All Weather) overfly the Empire State Building in the spring of 1948. Lt. Colonel Royal N. Baker was the CO at this time. Later, during the Korean War, he acquired 13 aerial kills. Twenty years later, he became vice commander of ADC from 2 January 1973 to 1 August 1975 as a Lt. General. (USAF)

Northrop Black Widow patch. (Marty Isham Collection)

This 5th FS (AW) F-61B, 43-8275, still sports its old "Pursuit" buzz number on 18 September 1948, at a Westover AFB open house in Massachusetts. Note the well-worn leading edges of the aircraft's twin vertical stabilizers. (H. Wood)

After serious problems with the P-82's Allison V-1710 engines, which proved to be inadequate for the airplane, ADC was willing to take its chances on the Twin Mustang because it desperately needed a replacement for the P-61s. The P-82 was expected to fly at more than 400 mph and have a service ceiling of more than 35,000 feet. With engines to be modified at squadron level, by mid 1949 all the aircraft were delivered to ADC's five squadrons as replacements for the tired Black Widows. History will kindly judge the Twin Mustang as a tremendously capable airplane conceived at the end of World War II for a mission that no longer really existed in the 1950s. Only about 60 of the newly designated F-82s were assigned to ADC, and were going to the salvage yard with less than 1,000 hours of flight time.

A nice lineup of 325th FTR GP (AW) at McChord AFB, Washington, during fall 1948. F-82F, 46-420, had been delivered in September that year. In June 1951 the airplane went to Brooks AFB, Texas, and was salvaged with only 746 flying hours. (B. Esposito)

In May 1950, F-94As began to arrive at McChord AFB to replace the Twin Mustangs. F-82F, 46-418, of the 318th, is shown in formation with new 318th F-94As. FQ-418 went to Brooks AFB on 5 August 1950 with only 550 hours total time. (USAF)

Cumulus Woody, *also a 319th FS (AW) F-82F. Photo possibly taken at Moses Lake AFB, Washington, in fall 1949.* (Via D. Menard)

Close-up of the Cumulus Woody *nose art, a take-off of the popular cartoon character Woody Woodpecker, reflects a new and more contemporary artistic style being applied to combat aircraft after World War II.* (Via D. Menard)

F-82F, 46-494, of the 319th FS (AW), shows off her clean lines on the McChord AFB ramp in 1949. Wing tank trim was blue, white, and red. *(Via D. Menard)*

Major W. H. Powell delivered the first Twin Mustang to the 52nd FG (AW) at Mitchel AFB on 22 June 1948. F-82B, 44-65177, would be used primarily for maintenance instruction. The aircraft is shown here on the Mitchel ramp in November 1948. Although the base was eventually closed due to encroaching suburbia in 1961, the original hangar in the background survived to became a part of the famed Long Island Cradle of Aviation Museum located there today. (USAF)

Sitting parked on the Mitchel AFB ramp is F-82F, 46-415. She was delivered on 9 September 1949 and deployed in May 1950 to the McClellan depot to be upgraded to an F-82G configuration. (M. Olmsted)

Colonel William Cellini, CO of the 52nd FAW GP at Mitchel AFB, has his personal aircraft on the Nellis AFB, Nevada, ramp during the 1950 USAF Worldwide Gunnery Meet on 26 March 1950. (W. T. Larkins)

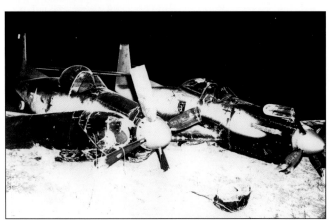

F-82F, 46-458, stalled while on approach to McGuire AFB, New Jersey. This rare and low-quality photo shows it crashed near Wrightstown, New Jersey, on 2 May 1950. Fortunately, both crew members walked away with only minor injuries. (USAF)

A 14th Fighter Group Republic F-47N, FE-416, from Dow AFB, Maine, flies over the Maine woods late in 1948. (USAF)

Republic F-47N Thunderbolt, buzz number FE-417, banks away from the camera, showing interesting oil and residue patterns on its belly caused by slipstream blowback. If this oil wasn't there, it meant that something was wrong with the engine! (USAF)

With snow-blowing crews in action in the background, a 14th FG, F-47N, taxis on the snowy Dow AFB ramp in late 1948. (USAF)

A beautiful left-side view of the CO's F-47D of the 47th FIS out of Niagara Falls, flown in for the Detroit Air Show in July 1953. Yellow cowling scallop and rudder tip, red fuselage stripes, and olive drab fuselage top and belly. (B. Baker)

Right side of the 47th FIS CO's F-47D. This aircraft has "True Blue" wingtips. Note the sharply stenciled air-craft number on the main landing gear door. (B. Baker)

At Selfridge AFB, Michigan, in August 1949, the 56th FG is using F-51Hs for target tugs. This is 44-64572 showing off her clean lines with high-visibility yellow on the prop spinner, wingtips, and tail area. (Wm. Balogh via Barbier Collection)

On 13 April 1953, FF-773, an RF-51D Mustang with CO's stripes of the 37th FIS from Ethan Allen AFB, Vermont, had a bit of a problem during a forced emergency landing in a field near Presque Isle AFB, Maine. (Thomas)

This target tug F-51D from the 4750th Air Base Squadron (Gunnery Training) from Yuma Arizona Training Center had a problem after its left main landing gear collapsed on landing in 1952. She would be repaired and go on to the ANG after the Korean War. (J. Eastham)

Chapter Two

A late-1947 or early-1948 photo of the 49th FS P-84Bs cruising over the scenic Maine countryside. Itsy Bitsy was being flown by Lt. Colonel George Laven, the 49th CO. This P-84B was salvaged on 15 April 1949. The emblem above the wing was never approved. (USAF)

Flying in the "Blowtorch Era"

F-80 Shooting Star, F-84 Thunderjet, F-86 Sabre, F-89 Scorpion, F-94 Starfire

Before there were swept-wing jet fighters capable of flying at Mach 1 in level flight, the first generation of production jets was known as the airplanes of the "Blowtorch Era." Despite having impressive names like Shooting Star, Thunderjet, Scorpion, and Starfire, these were all straight-wing subsonic aircraft.

Thunderjets in Air Defense! The 14th Fighter Group at Dow AFB took operational delivery of the first Republic P-84Bs in the USAF on 7 November 1947. Starting in the spring of 1948, these new aircraft were seen at numerous air shows in the United States, where the Air Force loved to show them to an adoring public. The colorful 37th Fighter Squadron (jet propelled) is seen here at the 1948 National Air Races in Cleveland, Ohio. This 37th aircraft sports a new squadron emblem to reflect the Jet Age. The emblem was never approved. (W. J. Balogh, Sr.)

This F-84B of the 49th FS at the 1948 National Air Races shows that the crew chief chopped off part of the "P" of the buzz number to make an "F". The 14th FG and its three FSs were inactivated on 2 October 1949 because of a USAF reduction in the budget. (W. J. Balogh, Sr.)

On 1 December 1948, the 33rd Fighter Group at Otis AFB was transferred to ADC from SAC with F-84Cs. This is the first F-84C ever built, and it was assigned to the 58th FS in the spring of 1949. (Via D. Menard)

The next Air Defense F-84 unit was the 78th Fighter Group at Hamilton AFB. In February 1949, F-84Ds began to arrive for the 82nd, 83rd, and 84th FS. These newly delivered F-84Ds sit on the Hamilton ramp in early March 1949. (USAF)

In the spring of 1950, this F-84D of the 78th FG sits on the Wold-Chamberlain Field ramp. Note the 78th FG emblem on the tail above the two diagonal red stripes. (Logan Coombs)

A four-ship formation of F-84Ds from the 78th FG flies together. Note that the F-84D in the foreground has three stripes on the tail and a three-color nose scalloping of red, white, and blue. (USAF)

In summer 1948, just prior to the 1 December 1948 transfer from SAC, these P-80s from the 27th FS sit on the ramp at March AFB, California. Nose, tanks, and tail markings are yellow. (USAF)

P-80A, PN-111, from the 71st FS suffered some belly landing damage on 30 August 1947. The 71st had blue markings. (USAF via D. Barbier)

In the spring of 1949 this 334th F-80 has the new buzz number of FT instead of PN. (Larkins)

Captain Vermont Garrison used this 335th FS F-80A during UHF testing in early 1949. (USAF)

A 336th FS F-80A sits on the Langley AFB ramp during the summer of 1948. Note the blue tail band and blue on the rear of the wing tank. (Larkins)

On 1 December 1948, the 56th FG at Selfridge AFB was transferred to ADC from SAC. The 61st, 62nd, and 63rd FSs were assigned F-80s. This F-80A of the 61st FS sports the flags of the FOX ABLE mission to Europe in July 1948. FT-041 was on display at the National Air Races at Cleveland in September 1949. Note that instead of the normal wing tank, a practice 100-pound yellow-painted bomb is mounted in its place. This is a Headquarters aircraft with red nose and tail band, white trim, and number 5. (W. J. Balogh, Sr., via Barbier)

In the summer of 1950, this 62nd FS F-80A awaits her next mission from the Selfridge AFB ramp. The nose and the forward part of the wing tank is painted red with the tail band and rear of the tank in yellow with black trim and number 45. (W. J. Balogh, Sr., via Barbier)

Also in the summer of 1950, this 63rd FS, F-80A shows her clean lines and attractive paint scheme. The nose, forward part of the wing tank, and tail band is a medium blue. The rear of the wing tank is red with a white division line and white trim on the tail band with a white number 64. (W. J. Balogh, Sr.)

In the spring of 1953, these F-80s sit on the Dow AFB ramp. The 49th FIS received the F-80s from the 132nd FIS Maine ANG on 1 November 1952 when the 49th was reactivated to replace the 132nd from its Korean call-up. (Bob Lilley via Bill Green)

With the Boeing facilities in the Northwest, the 325th Fighter Group at McChord AFB received its F-94As starting on 26 May 1950. Boeing let its Washington, D.C., reps know its frustration about the lack of decent air defense. The 317th, 318th, and 319th FSs rapidly replaced their F-82s with the F-94As. Here is the 318th Fighter All-Weather Squadron (FAWS) and the CO's aircraft, the last F-94A, in the spring of 1950. Three yellow stripes are behind the canopy, yellow trim on the wing tank, the World War II 318th emblem on the fuselage, and the 325th FG emblem on the tail. (USAF via J. Wogstad)

The 325th FG CO's aircraft sits on the McChord AFB ramp in the spring of 1950. (K. Keaveney Collection)

F-94As of the 319th or 317th FAWS appear to be en route to gunnery practice over the southwestern United States. (K. Keaveney Collection)

The 52nd FG at McGuire AFB was the second unit to receive the F-94A in October 1950 to replace its F-82s. Here is the group CO's aircraft in summer 1951. Note the colors of the arrow on the nose representing the 2nd and 5th FSs. (J. Redrup)

On Armed Forces Day 1952, this F-94A of the 2nd FIS sits proudly on display. The nose of the jet carries the red arrow and red circle around the unique 2nd FIS emblem. (B. Esposito)

In the summer of 1952, this 2nd FIS F-94A gets refueled at McGuire AFB. (R. Uppstrom)

The 61st FIS at Selfridge AFB received its first two F-94Bs on 23 March 1951. This F-94B of "B" flight denoted by the white band on the tank, is seen here soon after its arrival. (W. J. Balogh, Sr., via Barbier)

Various USAF histories and publications denote that the 61st FIS received the first F-94Bs. However, aircraft record cards of the F-94B show that the 59th FIS at Otis AFB received its first two F-94Bs on 17 March 1951, one on the 19th, two on the 20th, and one more on the 21st. In this photo two F-94Bs of the 59th FIS fly over Cape Cod; FA-870 wears the three yellow stripes of the CO's aircraft in the spring of 1951. (USAF)

The next blowtorch-era interceptor was the Northrop F-89B, when four arrived at the 84th FIS at Hamilton AFB on 21 June 1951. The first XF-89 had flown back on 16 August 1948, but the Scorpion program encountered extensive developmental problems. The 83rd FIS at Hamilton also received the initial F-89Bs. Both squadrons were under the 78th Fighter Interceptor Wing at Hamilton. These F-89Bs were on the Hamilton ramp in late 1951 with the 84th colors of yellow with black trim. Note the small scorpion in the tail band of 471 and the 78th FIWg emblem in the tail band of 54, with the 84th FIS emblem on the nose. (J. Balzer Collection)

In the summer of 1952, an F-89C of the 84th FIS prepares for takeoff on a training mission. Note the power cart has an 84th Fighter Squadron emblem stencil. (J. Balzer Collection)

On 3 July 1952, this 84th FIS F-89B encountered a landing gear problem at Hamilton AFB. (J. Balzer Collection)

During the spring of 1953, this 433rd FIS F-89C shows off its shark mouth. The tail emblem is a red F-89 with a scorpion tail over clouds and yellow lightning bolts. Later this aircraft would leave the 433rd to be refurbished at the factory and assigned to the 65th FIS in Alaska, at Elmendorf AFB. It crashed on 29 October 1953. (W. J. Balogh, Sr., via Menard)

During the summer of 1954, this F-89C from the 433rd FIS is on display, sporting a very cool-looking paint job. (D. Menard)

The F-94C entered the inventory on 10 March 1953, with the 437th FIS at Otis AFB. Major "Chappie" James is the squadron commander, freshly back from the Korean War. This picture shows Chappie leading a four-ship formation over Cape Cod in Chappie's Chariot. Stripes on the fuselage and wing tanks are green. (USAF)

The Operations Officer of the 437th FIS has his F-94C on display at a 1954 Open House at Otis AFB. Two stripes on the aircraft denote the OPSO, or Operations Officer. (R. Willet)

A 29th FIS F-94C shows off her markings at the National Air Show at Tinker AFB. The display was from 1 to 3 September 1956. Numerous USAF squadrons lined the ramp. Based at Malmstrom AFB, Montana, that arctic red tail was eye-catching in the winter snows. (Via M. Bacon)

The ramp at Malmstrom AFB has 29th FIS F-94Cs ready to go during the summer of 1956. (W. Johnson)

A 332nd FIS F-94C is on the Nellis AFB, Nevada, ramp in December 1954. She's a long way from her home at New Castle County Airport in Delaware. The four red stripes denote the 525th Air Defense Group CO's aircraft. (C. Burns)

Falcon and Scorpions

A modified Northrop F-89D was the initial carrier of the Hughes Falcon, and the first firing on 21 October 1953 was not too successful because the missile pod collapsed after launch. The necessary redesign set back the production date of the Falcon-equipped F-89Hs from January 1954 to late-1955.

Finally, on 27 January 1955, a fully armed Falcon fired from another modified F-89D successfully shot down a Boeing QB-17 Drone. This was the first GAR-1 missile armed with an active warhead to ever strike an airborne aircraft.

The F-89D joined the blowtorch era on 7 January 1954, when the 18th FIS at Minneapolis-St Paul Airport got its first Scorpions. The squadron wouldn't be there long, as they would be transferred to the Alaskan Air Command on 1 September 1954 at Ladd AFB near Fairbanks. This picture shows a 58th FIS F-89D from Otis AFB at the National Air Show at Philadelphia, Pennsylvania, in September 1955. (W. M. Jeffries)

The 318th FIS F-89D from Presque Isle AFB is on the 138th FIS ramp for Armed Forces Day 1955 at Syracuse, New York. Note the colorful wing tank markings. (D. L. Borne)

This 321st FIS F-89D, out of Paine Field, Washington, flies over the cloud-covered Cascade Mountains of the Northwest during spring 1956. The rocket pod markings are shown to good advantage and the 321st emblem is on the tail. (J. Ford)

A 437th FIS F-89D, from Oxnard AFB, California, sits on the Nellis AFB ramp in the summer of 1956. The yellow-and-black markings are very eye-catching. (Via L. Davis)

The final Scorpion model produced by Northrop was the F-89H and it arrived to the blowtorch era two years late, in March 1956. The 445th FIS at Wurtsmith AFB, Michigan, was the first H squadron. ADC's F-89Hs would have a short life as the ANG began to receive them in November. This 76th FIS F-89H is on the Ethan Allen AFB in the summer of 1959. (USAF)

An F-89H of the 84th FIS taxis at its home base of Hamilton AFB in the summer of 1956. Note the 78th Fighter Group emblem in the tail band. (W. M. Jeffries)

A 437th FIS F-89H from Oxnard AFB, California, sits on the Edwards AFB ramp in the fall of 1956. Note the D markings carried over to the H. The tiger emblem of the 437th adorns the tail. (N. Filer)

Looking almost radioactive, this 432nd FIS F-89H sits in the glow of the "live" atomic warhead-equipped Genie missile shot of 19 July 1957 (background, right). The H is sitting on the Indian Springs Auxiliary Airfield ramp. An 84th FIS F-89J fired the Genie, the "John Shot" of Operation Plumb Bob. (Isham Collection)

USAF historical writings indicate that the first F-89J squadron was the 84th FIS at Hamilton AFB in January 1957. Here is a picture taken in early spring 1957. (A. Berry)

At the 1958 William Tell competition, a 29th FIS weapon crew prepares to load a Genie missile. This competition featured the first competitive use of the missile. The arctic-red tails and wing tanks of the 29th FIS were very distinctive on the ramp at Tyndall AFB, Texas. (USAF)

Sitting on the ramp at Ellsworth AFB, South Dakota, is a 54th FIS F-89J in 1958. The F-89J was a modified F-89D; 350 aircraft were so done. The J had the Hughes MG-12 fire-control system, and could carry two MB-1s, later redesignated AIR-2As, Genie air-to-air rockets. The F-89J was the first USAF nuclear-armed interceptor and could also carry four Falcons. (Via B. Curry Collection)

At the 1959 William Tell competition, the 319th FIS showed up in its F-89s sporting a dark blue-and-white color scheme. The "Tomcats" (no relation to the later F-14) captured first place in the F-89 category with 4,900 points. Note the snazzy-looking whitewall tires! (Via Dave Ostrowski)

A very unique F-89D. The "Norcrafters," employees of Northrop, had amassed enough accident-free hours to buy an F-89D. This aircraft has been wheeled out to the 89D line at the Palmdale, California, facility. Except for the nose and the vertical stabilizer tip, the aircraft is totally white with the green cross-and-circle safety emblem. (Via T. Chong Collection)

Chapter Three

The Yuma range hosted the 465th FIS from McChord AFB in 1954. FU-078 is flying in those clear Arizona skies. (K. Lotz)

Supersonic Sabres (...Only in a Dive)

F-86D Sabre Dog

As good as the North American F-86 Sabre Jet was as a dog-fighter in the skies over Korea, the airplane needed improvement to become an effective interceptor. A radar nose gave the jet all-weather capability, while an uprated turbojet engine with afterburner provided the necessary power for alert "scrambles."

The F-86A Sabre arrived to ADC at Langley AFB to the 4th Fighter Group on 6 June 1949. Finally ADC had a superior interceptor, as those swept wings made the Sabre a "hot" aircraft. It pushed Mach 1 in level flight and could break the sound barrier, but only in a dive. Not long after delivery, the 335th FS formed an aerobatic team with its new Sabres. With the highly polished natural-metal aircraft, it was easy to name the team: The Silver Sabres. This aircraft was at the Cleveland National Air Race in September 1949. Note excessive paint wear on the nose from airloads. A little more than a year later, the 4th would be notified of a move to Korea on 8 November 1950, where the wing would make history. (W. J. Balogh, Sr., via Menard)

On 1 April 1950, the 1st Fighter Group was transferred from TAC to ADC with the 27th, 71st, and 94th FISs. This early 27th FIS photo shows a staged scramble for the photographer. Note the power cart for only the closest airplane is plugged in but its canopy is still closed. (USAF)

Effective 15 August 1950, the 27th FIS relocated to Griffiss AFB, New York. This December 1951 photo shows a 27th Sabre about to depart on a sortie. (I. Clark)

The 27th FIS came under the 4711th Defense Wing on 6 February 1952, and by early spring the "California" markings were replaced by new markings of yellow band with three black stars and black trim. (R. Gil)

71st FIS Sabres line the George AFB ramp in early spring 1950. The 71st would move to Griffiss AFB on 15 August 1950 and then to Greater Pittsburgh Airport on 21 August 1950. This East Coast shuffling was brought about by the 4th Fighter Wing's Korean deployment. (USAF)

On 15 February 1949, the first four F-86As were delivered to the 94th FIS at March AFB. By late summer this F-86A, 58-130, sits for her portrait with 206-gallon ferry tanks. (USAF)

F-86A, FU-130, from the right side. Early colors were beautiful back in 1949. (H. G. Martin)

On 18 July 1950, the 94th FIS relocated to George AFB, California. This December 1951 photo shows early markings, just the 94th emblem. (B. Butcher)

By June 1953, the 94th F-86As were flying around the Southern California skies with these notable markings. (B. Butcher)

This 49th FIS F-86F was a long way from Dow AFB during the summer of 1953. It was transient at Kirtland AFB, New Mexico. The white stars denote the 4711th Defense Wing. (Via G. Olvera)

Colonel Harrison Thyng, CO of the Hq. 33rd Fighter Interceptor Wing at Otis AFB, has taxied in after a training mission. His F-86A has the red, yellow, and blue color bands of the 58th, 59th, and 60th FISs. It appears that the tail marks and fuselage lightning bolt are the red of the 58th FIS. Colonel Thyng was CO of the Headquarters 33rd from April 1951 to October 1951. He commanded the 4th FIWg in Korea from 1 November 1951 to 2 October 1952 and achieved five MiG kills. (USAF)

Colonel Thyng shares a joke with his crew chief, TSgt. Salvatore Latona, before a mission. Note the three squadron colors on his helmet. Also note that the data block shows F-86A-5-NA and 49-1122-A. (USAF)

A right-side view of a 60th FIS F-86A, FU-143. Note the 33rd Fighter Interceptor Group insignia behind the jammed gun door. (R. Willett)

This nice 62nd FIS F-86A, 49-1010, photo was taken in the summer of 1950 at O'Hare Airport in Chicago, Illinois. Note the two bands denoting the Operations Officer's aircraft. (R. W. Casey)

On 3 December 1950, this color photo appeared in the Detroit News as a black-and-white picture. Members of the 63rd FIS stand tall in front of their F-86As for an inspection. Exact date of this rare color photograph is unknown. (C. W. King)

The 75th FIS relocated to Suffolk County AFB, New York, from Dow AFB, effective 16 October 1952. It looks like not too soon after the move, the CO of the 75th FIS, in his F-86A, 49-1280, finds himself in formation over the Great South Bay with a U.S. Navy Grumman F9F-6 Cougar. The Cougar appears to be "fresh off the line" from Grumman's Bethpage, Long Island, facility. (U.S. Navy)

A view of 84th FIS F-86Fs. The 84th competed against the 60th FIS with F-86Es, the 93rd FIS with F-86As, the 318th with F-94As, and the 354th FIS with F-51Ds. And the winner was...the 354th FIS with its Mustangs! This aerial gunnery meet, the first for ADC, was held from 5 to 10 March 1953 at Yuma, Arizona. (USAF)

Also during the summer of 1951 the 93rd FIS, with its F-86As from Larson AFB, Washington, deployed to Bentwaters, England. The temporary duty (TDY) assignment became a permanent change of station (PCS) to USAF Europe (USAFE).
(L. Davis Collection)

Based at Kirtland AFB, the 93rd FIS, with its F-86As, protected the atomic facilities at Los Alamos. The 93rd began to receive Sabres in October 1949. By the end of January 1954, the F-86D replaced the F-86As. The 93rd Sabres carried red-and-white bands on the nose and tail. (USAF)

During the fall of 1951, the 93rd FIS participated in B-36 intercept tests. Different color bands were painted on its Sabres. F-86A 48-133 was a test aircraft. (R. Escola)

This 97th FIS F-86E, 51-2845, from Wright-Patterson AFB, Ohio, is escorting a B-50 over the Ohio countryside in June 1953. (Picciani Aircraft Slides)

In the spring of 1954 the 330th FIS at Stewart AFB, New York, was flying F-86Fs. The five-star pattern denotes the 4709th Defense Wing. F-86F, 51-13383, also has the dark-green and white nose and tail markings. Note the 330th emblem over the wing. (H. Carter)

This photo showing a 539th FIS F-86F, FU-3111, was also taken in the summer of 1954. This unit was based at Stewart AFB, NY. (Milton Riggs)

Another 539th view of F-86F FU-3111. (Milton Riggs)

On 16 July 1953, F-86D, 51-6145, carrying a full rocket load, set a new world speed record of 715.697 mph.

Lt. Colonel William Barnes, an Air Materiel Command production test pilot, entered the Salton Sea course in a dive in full afterburner. Also, the air temperature was 105 degrees F and sonic speed at this temperature would be 797 mph. Only the F-100 Super Sabre could break the speed of sound in level flight. All ADC Sabres would have to be in a dive. None of the Dogs had manual fuel control; they were all the same in that respect, no matter what dash number. They all had electronic fuel control with variable area exhaust nozzle and afterburner. You could bypass the electronic fuel control by flipping a toggle switch from normal to emergency, which put you on the emergency fuel-control system, controlled manually by the throttle.

The emergency system was never used except in emergencies and sometimes for starting. To avoid hot starts and to save engines, standard operating procedure (SOP) was to use manual start only, bypassing the electronic fuel control. (Overnight condensation sometimes caused a short circuit in the black box and you could get an overtemperature condition—more than 1,000 degrees F—when using an automatic start.) Once the engine was running, the situation was less critical and the electronic fuel control could be cut back in, as it was probably dried out by then.

Incidentally, the throttle could be moved in afterburner range, varying the afterburner thrust; unlike the F-94 afterburner, which was either on or off. As for the bugs being ironed out of the electronic fuel control—they never really were. It worked fine when it worked, but it didn't work a lot of the time, and ADC lost a lot of engines and had a lot of down time on the F-86Ds because of it.

The 94th FIS at George AFB received ADC's first F-86D on 10 February 1953. This arrival was almost two years behind schedule because of the E-4 fire-control system and problems with the General Electric J47-GE-17 turbojet engine. This picture shows F-86D-25s shortly after arrival to the 94th in March 1953. By 30 June 1953, seventeen F-86Ds were assigned. (USAF)

The 49th FIS has an F-86D on display during an open house in 1955, perhaps at its home, Dow AFB. This flight lead's aircraft carries green tail and nose bands with three white stars. The green fuselage band has black trim. In October 1956 the 49th received ADC's first F-86Ls at Hanscom Field, Massachusetts. (T. Cuddy)

This 5th FIS F-86D was shot in November 1955, possibly at Suffolk County AFB. Star layout on the tail signifies the 4709th Air Defense Wing. Each star is for an FIS assigned to the wing. (E. Bosetti)

The 13th FIS was flying F-86Ds out of Selfridge AFB at the time of this picture, around December 1953. The red-and-white shooting-star tail marking denotes the 4708th Defense Wing. The angry bull emblem of the 13th is over the wing. (USAF)

Mid-1957 has this 15th FIS F-86D in the Arizona sky near Davis-Monthan AFB, Arizona. In August 1957 F-86Ls began to arrive. The 15th had received its F-86Ds back in February 1954. (R. Waddell)

During the February/March 1955 time frame, the 37th FIS from Ethan Allen AFB deployed to Yuma for rocketry training. Back on 4 September 1953, the first two F-86Ds had arrived to the 37th. Here a flight lead aircraft gets some work done on the Yuma ramp. Prior to the deployment, arctic red had been applied to all the F-86Ds. (USAF Via John Dennison)

37th FIS squadron commander, Major Dave Severen, stands by the squadron's car during the Yuma deployment. From nearby at the Canadian border in Vermont to almost the Mexican border in Arizona, the round trip sure put some miles on the Ford's odometer! (USAF)

F-86Ls arrived to the 94th in October 1956. This picture shows the F-86Ls in March 1958 during a stop-over at Kirtland AFB. They were heading back to the cold ramp at Selfridge from live-fire training at Vincent AFB, Arizona. 30th Air Division emblems are on the tails. (Bruder)

Under gleaming hangar lighting, an 85th FIS F-86D at Scott AFB, Illinois, is open for display on 18 May 1957. Note the colorful wing tank painted white with blue, white, and red trim. The fin is blue with white stars to match the tail markings. (Dave Ostrowski)

Road Runner, *an F-86D of the 97th FIS, sits on her home base ramp at Wright-Patterson AFB in 1954.* (D. N. Drew)

In the spring of 1955, a 323rd FIS F-86D at Larson AFB shows off her markings. The 323rd emblem is on the center of the fuselage. On 18 August 1955, the 323rd designation would go to Truax AFB, Wisconsin. (H. P. Saabye)

A "Sabre Knights" F-86D from Hamilton AFB is shown at the Detroit, Michigan, airport on 4 July 1955. This was ADC's premier aerobatic team. (D. Menard)

During the 4 July 1957 open house at George AFB, Sweet Mudder of the 329th FIS shows off her colorful markings for the crowd. The two white diagonal stripes on the nose denotes the jet as the OPS Officer's aircraft. (Yocum)

This F-86D of the 332nd FIS out of McGuire AFB is shown flying over the Yuma range in 1956. (Brown)

The 432nd FIS at Truax AFB received its first F-86Ds on 10 June 1953. This photo was possibly taken in late 1953 on a training sortie out of Truax. (W. Gatschet)

Renowned aviation photographer, historian, and author Peter Bowers shot this 497th FIS Dog at Larson AFB in late summer 1955. The black-and-white marks on the tail and nose are ex-445th FIS markings. (P. Bowers)

This shark-mouth F-86D is from the 520th FIS at Geiger Field in the spring of 1955. Note the light snow on the ramp and surrounding areas. Dark blue with white stars motif is shown on the canopy rail and tail. The nine stars on the tail are for the 9th Air Division. The three stripes denote the squadron CO's aircraft. Wing tank marks are red, white, and blue. The shark mouth is red with white teeth and black trim. After the 18 August 1955 reorganization, a tiger head was put on the top of the tail, over the stars for the 498th FIS. (USAF)

After the 18 August 1955 reorganization, the 539th FIS was flying ex-5th FIS aircraft at McGuire AFB. Here is the CO's aircraft in the fall of 1955, with a blue tail with white stars and trim and three red fuselage stripes. Note 539th emblem on the nose. (Sommerich)

In February 1957, the 42nd FIS began to receive F-86Ls. On 1 December 1957, the 42nd ceased alert operations. The aircraft were flown out to the ANG and this F-86L of the 42nd was shot on the Kansas ramp. (Via J. Geer)

F-86Ls began to arrive to the 83rd FIS at Hamilton AFB in April 1957. This L of the 83rd was photographed on 15 September 1957 at NAS Oakland. (W. T. Larkins)

The 444th FIS at Charleston AFB, South Carolina, began receiving F-86Ls in March 1957. This shot of FU-047 appears to have been taken that summer. Note the flight lead's fuselage band is golden yellow with black trim behind the "U.S." The 444th would begin McDonnell F-101B deliveries in March 1960. (USAF)

In August 1957 F-86Ls began to arrive to the 456th FIS at Castle AFB, California. This superb photo was taken early in 1958. On 8 February 1958 the F-86Ls were off alert and the supersonic Convair F-102 Delta Dagger "Deuces" were soon to arrive. (K. W. Bell)

Chapter Four

A nice right-echelon formation photo of 538th FIS Starfighters in 1958. The "Zipper" always looked good in air-to-air shots. The 538th would give up its 104s in May 1960 and deactivate on 1 July 1960. (USAF)

The Century Series

F-101 Voodoo, F-102 Delta Dagger,
F-104 Starfighter, F-106 Delta Dart

The Air Force fighter matured to a new level of sophistication and performance in the mid-1950s with the advent of the famed Century Series. Most of these new airplanes went supersonic on their very first flights, and featured such items as Inertial Navigation Systems and advanced analog fire control systems.

Convair F-102A, 54-1379, arrives at George AFB on the afternoon of 24 April 1956. FC-379 ushered in the supersonic era to the 327th FIS and ADC. However, this was almost three years past the June 1953 production date written in the letter contract of December 1951, some seven months beyond a new and revised delivery schedule set in March 1954, and nearly 10 years after the experimental delta-wing XF-92A's first flight on 18 September 1948. In other words, the long-awaited USAF "1954 Interceptor" was two years late. F-102A, 54-1379, was conditionally accepted on 19 April 1956 at Palmdale, and then flown to nearby George AFB on 24 April. On 30 April it was formally signed over and assigned to the 327th FIS. (USAF)

Soon after arrival to the 327th FIS on 4 June 1956, F-102A, 54-1381, sits on the George AFB ramp for her portrait. Note the placement of the early F-102 markings and lettering. (Budd Butcher)

As with any new USAF aircraft, HQ USAF would put it on display to show how the nation's defense dollars were being spent. Soon after delivery, the 327th sent six F-102s to the National Air Show at Oklahoma City's Will Rogers Airport from 1-3 September 1956. The squadron's CO, Lt. Colonel Charles E. Regney, had his personal aircraft, the Purina Checkerboard Special, *on display. It was F-102A, 54-1396.* (Budd Butcher)

A close-up of the unique checkerboard pattern on the tail of Lt. Colonel Regney's Duece as displayed at the 1956 National Air Show. Split speed brake can be seen in the open position directly above the engine exhaust. (Budd Butcher)

After the arrival and placement of his Deuce, Lt. Colonel Charles E. Regney proudly stands by for an informal portrait. Note that the band of flight colors go under the belly of his aircraft. (Budd Butcher)

In mid-February 1958, the 327th was notified that they would leave warm, sunny George AFB in California and be reassigned to Thule AB, Greenland. The squadron arrived at Thule on 6 July 1958, led by Major Ted Adams, 327th CO. Hangar space at Thule dictated that only thirteen Deuces could be assigned. More than 60 Deuces had been assigned at George AFB. The 327th had left George AFB on 24 June 1958. In August 1958, a trio of Deuces overfly the Wolstenholm Fjord. (Budd Butcher)

It is February 1959 and -35 degrees F. The Deuces and pilots of the 327th, however, are ready to scramble. Even though the 327th had been the first Deuce FIS squadron and had literally "written the book" on Deuce operations, it was not saved from being inactivated. On 16 February 1960, the "Iron Men" ceased alert operations and on 25 March 1960, the squadron was inactivated at Thule. Note that the 327th suffered no F-102 losses, even with 61 of the new jets having been assigned. (Budd Butcher)

An 11th FIS Deuce heads out for a training mission at Duluth Airport in 1959. The 11th flew Deuces from August 1956 to June 1960. (J. Geer Collection)

This 18th FIS F-102A is at the Armed Force Day in May 1959 at Wurtsmith AFB. The diagonal stripe on the tail is yellow, bordered in white. (W. J. Balogh Sr.)

A 47th FIS from Niagara Falls Airport is towed out for an air show in 1959. The tail band is yellow, bordered in black. (Fred T. Guthrie via D. Slowiak)

Showing a light blue-and-white checkerboard pattern on its rudder, this Deuce returns from a cold air defense mission in the spring of 1968 at Keflavik, Iceland. This rudder pattern was not used for very long. (USAF)

A bit south of its home at Goose Bay AB, Labrador, Canada, this TF-102A of the 59th FIS sits on the Andrews AFB, Maryland, transient ramp on 19 June 1965. The 59th flew the Deuce out of Goose Bay from May 1960 to December 1966. (J. G. Handleman)

Showing a 327th Fighter Group emblem on its tail, a Deuce of the 61st FIS out of Truax Field is open for inspection on 21 May 1960. (B. Knowles Collection)

A 64th FIS Deuce sits on the Paine Field ramp soon after arrival in March 1960 from McChord AFB. (D. Barbier Collection)

In early April 1966, these Deuces from the 64th FIS out of Paine Field, overfly the picturesque Washington coastline prior to the 64th's Southeast Asia deployment in June. (USAF)

A 76th FIS Deuce is put on display at Andrews AFB in 1961. The 76th was based at Westover AFB. (T. Cuddy)

Now with red-and-white tail markings, this Deuce of the 76th FIS is seen in October 1962. (Ron Harrison)

This TF-102A of the 86th FIS is on the ramp line in the summer of 1959 at Youngstown Municipal Airport, Ohio. A red lightning bolt is on the rudder. The 86th was at Youngstown from 1 November 1952 to its inactivation on 1 March 1960. (R. Ruhue)

A 95th FIS pilot confers with his crew chief at Andrews AFB prior to a mission in March 1958. The 95th wouldn't have the Deuce for long, as the F-106 Delta Dart would arrive in July 1959. (USAF)

This trio of 318th FIS Deuces is overflying the Puget Sound area near McChord AFB in the summer of 1958. FC-425 would later crash with the 64th FIS out of Paine Field on 15 October 1963. (USAF)

During the summer of 1958, this 318th Deuce awaits its next mission. (D. Barbier Collection)

A 325th FIS Deuce has taxied in from a mission during exercise Swift Strike III in July 1963. The 325th from Truax Field were staging out of McEntire ANGB, South Carolina. The 327th Fighter Group emblem is on the tail. Note the Day Glo stripes area also on the wing. The 325th was the interceptor force of the "Red" air force. (J. Wogstad Collection)

A new emblem was approved in 1961 for the "Sky Wolves" and is seen on this 326th FIS Deuce in May 1964. (J. Geer)

Here is a 329th FIS Deuce from George AFB at a May 1959 open house at Long Beach Airport. The tail marking was later carried over to its F-106s. (Harry Gann)

Sitting on the McCarran Field ramp on 21 September 1962 is a 331st FIS F-102A from Webb AFB, Texas. The Deuce was loaned to the 199th FIS, Hawaii ANG, for the 1962 Ricks Trophy Race, hence the 199th emblem (above the numeral "6") on the tail. (Douglas D. Olson)

A 332nd FIS is being moved on the McGuire AFB ramp in 1958. The "new" 332nd emblem is on both sides of the tail. The next year, in July, the 332nd moved to England AFB, Louisiana, and then, one year later, in July 1960, relocated to Thule AB. (Via J. Geer)

This 438th FIS F-102A is at the Fargo, North Dakota, ANG base in the summer of 1958. The 438th didn't really have any spectacular marks, just the 438th emblem on the left side and the 507th Fighter Group emblem on the right side of the tail. (ND ANG Photo via D. Slowiak)

April 1963 shows this 460th FIS Deuce sitting on the Portland ramp after a rain shower or two. The squadron emblem was spectacular and was on both sides of the tail. The 460th flew Deuces from May 1958 to March 1966. (R. Lawson Collection)

During the Cuban Missile Crisis, the 482nd FIS from Seymour Johnson AFB, North Carolina, deployed into Homestead AFB, Florida. This 482nd Deuce is ready for its next combat air patrol. Note the tower shows a 7-foot elevation. (USAF)

An early 498th FIS F-102 taxies by white fence dividing the civilian area from the military ramp on Geiger Field, Washington, as a commercial Douglas DC-3 lands in the background. Note small "star and bar" on the forward nose and how U.S. Air Force lettering curves down the air intake trunk. (Ron Dupas, Barbier Collection)

Sporting a new paint job, this 73rd Air Division F-102A is over the Tyndall AFB gulf range in late 1960. This Deuce had previously flown with the 329th FIS. (USAF)

Air Defense Weapons Center "Tub," 56-2317, sitting parked on the Andrews AFB transient ramp in late 1968. (Frank MacSorley)

This 4780th Air Defense Wing (Training) Deuce at Perrin AFB sits on the Nellis AFB ramp on 21 September 1962. Note the 73rd Air Division emblem on the tail band as the 4780th was under the 73rd. (W. M. Jeffries)

Another Perrin AFB F-102A, also from the 4780th, sits on the transient ramp at Andrews AFB on 17 July 1970. This camouflaged Deuce is really clean. On 30 June 1971, Colonel Vermont Garrison, Wing Commander, brings to an end Deuce training at Perrin. The Deuces were flown out to ANG units. (Jack Morris)

The initial mockup inspection of the F-104 on 30 April 1953 led to the replacement of the two 30mm guns with one 20mm GE Gatling gun, the M-61 Vulcan cannon (at this time under development and then known as the T-171 gun) for a decrease in weight of 80 pounds. When finally fitted in the F-104, repeated failures in the flight testing of the gun led HQ USAF, in late 1957, to consider it too unreliable for the F-104. It was not until the ANG gave back to ADC its F-104s in 1963 that the M-61 would come back. The gun was fitted back in the F-104 as it was in 1964. From 1958 to 1964, only Sidewinders were carried for armament. F-104Bs didn't carry the gun, as the rear seat took up the M-61 space.

Two Lockheed F-104A Starfighters from the 83rd FIS at Hamilton AFB, California, are shown flying in tight echelon formation in early 1958. Note their gun ports are faired over indicating that the aircraft's M-61 Vulcan cannons had not been installed. Early-generation Philco-Bendix AIM-9 Sidewinder heat-seeking air-to-air missiles are mounted on the jets' wingtips as the primary means of destroying enemy aircraft. The 83rd FIS became the first ADC unit to fly the F-104 when Lt. Colonel Raymond E. Evans landed at Hamilton with a flight of three Starfighters on 12 January 1958. (USAF)

Sporting an 83rd FIS emblem, this YF-104A, 55-2969, takes to the air on 16 May 1958. Piloted by Captain Walter W. Irwin of the 83rd FIS, this YF-104A set a new speed record of 1,404.19 mph. This 104 was never assigned to the 83rd. (USAF)

83rd FIS personnel began their TDY to Formosa on 6 September 1958, "Project Jonah Able." This lasted until 5 December 1958, when the unit began deploying home after being replaced by 337th FIS personnel. Twelve F-104s were loaded in C-124s to be flown to Taoyuan Air Base, Formosa. This picture of the Flying Dutchman appears to have been taken in Formosa during that deployment. The 83rd flew the F-104 from January 1958 to August 1960. (S. B. Brown)

In the late summer of 1958, Starfighters of the 538th FIS at Larson AFB go through some maintenance before their next mission. The 538th received its F-104As in March 1958. (USAF)

With long-range wingtip tanks, these F-104As from the 538th FIS are seen on the ramp at Luke AFB, Arizona, in 1958. (D. Dickman)

This F-104A flying over the California high desert from Edwards AFB would be assigned to the 337th FIS on 23 May 1958 at Westover AFB. (USAF)

The 56th FIS at Wright-Patterson AFB converted from F-86Ls to F-104s and on 5 May 1958 received its first F-104A, 56-0756. This F-104A picture was taken not long after the aircraft arrived in October 1958. On 17 February 1960, the last 104 departed the 56th and the unit inactivated on 1 March 1960. (D. Menard)

In February 1962, HQ USAF ponders the thought that ANG FISs with F-104s be rotated through the Homestead alert facility. HQ ADC did not like this idea and came back with the counter idea to transfer all ANG F-104s back to ADC. This was workable. When this happened, HQ ADC now proposed to move the 71st FIS from Selfridge to Homestead and be assigned F-104s. Instead, DOD moved VF(AW)-3 with U.S. Navy Douglas F-4D Skyrays to Key West NAS from San Diego. One can only wonder if the 27th FIS at Loring AFB would have been moved to Selfridge if the 71st FIS had flown F-104s? On 1 March 1963, the 319th FIS relocated to Homestead AFB flying the F-104.

On 15 May 1965 at Patrick AFB, Florida, this 319th F-104A shows off a new paint job and the gun is not faired over. (Ben Knowles)

The 331st FIS at Webb AFB after flying F-102s, receives the F-104 on 9 May 1963. Lt. Colonel Jack Price flew in the first F-104. With white lightning bolts in the 331st emblem, this picture taken in May 1963 also has a golden-yellow bolt on a 331st Starfighter tail. (Via T. Landis)

In February 1964, GE/USAF teams finally begin to install the "new and improved" M-61 20mm Vulcan gun in the F-104. This impressive line-up of Starfighters was taken at Homestead AFB, Florida, on 6 June 1964 during gun installment. Note there are two F-104s with 331st FIS markings along with these 319th F-104s and not all are painted gray. While receiving guns, the 331st FIS pulled alert at Homestead. (Via T. Landis)

This is the right side of the airplanes in the picture above, showing 319th tail markings. (Via T. Landis)

The FAA did sonic boom tests on Oklahoma City, Oklahoma, from 3 February 1964 to 30 July 1964 for SST evaluation. The 331st FIS was involved with the test, doing eight sonic booms per day. A "Sooner Boomer" name tag was applied to the Starfighters. This picture shows FG-821 with the sun reflecting off its highly polished surface during a boom run. (USAF)

On 13 April 1965, this 331st FIS Starfighter was photographed at Webb AFB. Within two years, on 1 March 1967, the 331st would be inactivated with its F-104s and personnel going to the 4760th Combat Crew Training Squadron (CCTS). (Norm Taylor)

This picture shows 4760th CCTS Starfighters on the Peterson Field ramp on 25 August 1967. Note that the 331st emblem on the tail has been replaced by a 14th Air Force emblem. The primary mission of the 4760th was to train Jordanian pilots and maintenance crews in the F-104. The 4760th CCTS flew the Starfighter from 1 March 1967 to 31 December 1967, and was the last ADC squadron. (USAF)

The CO of the 4760th CCTS flew this F-104B into Maxwell AFB, Alabama, in 1967. ADC's 14th Air Force was headquartered there and was having a one-year anniversary party for being assigned to ADC on 1 April 1966. The shark's teeth were quite impressive! (Barry Miller)

It's the morning of the 5th of January 1959, on the McDonnell tarmac, and the first F-101B, 56-0281, will arrive to the 60th FIS at Otis AFB later that day. This Voodoo had been signed for on 2 January. Note that 60281 has red markings on the tail and fuselage, and that the 60th FIS emblem on the tail is not the usual crow emblem. Perhaps the squadron commander wanted a "new" emblem, with a "new" aircraft. (Don Wood Collection)

Showing off its new ADC lightning bolts tail marking, F-101B, 57-0376 heads out from Otis AFB over the Atlantic Ocean early in 1960. This Voodoo would be totaled after a mid-air collision with 57-0378, also with the 60th, near Dow AFB on 14 November 1967. (USAF)

This 60th FIS Voodoo is on display at Otis AFB during the May Armed Forces Day celebration in 1961. (Tom Cuddy)

Without a doubt, the 60th FIS commander wanted his Voodoo to be seen. His F-101B was at Hanscom AFB on 2 October 1965. On 1 April 1971, the 60th would cease alert operations and inactivate on 30 April 1971, the longest serving ADC Voodoo squadron. (Tom Cuddy)

Captain Al Roberts has shot off this MB-1 Genie at Tyndall and the USAF photographer has captured a stunning shot during a 2nd FIS weapons deployment from Suffolk County AFB. (USAF)

This beautiful portrait of a natural-metal 13th FIS was taken at Nellis AFB on 22 September 1962. The 13th was based at Glasgow AFB, Montana. (Doug Olson)

In 1964 the 13th FIS also participated in the "Sooner Boomer" sonic boom tests on Oklahoma City, Oklahoma, for future SST operations. (USAF)

During an open house in May 1961, the crew of this 15th FIS Voodoo tries some recruitment on a couple of future ADC pilots at Luke AFB. The 15th was based at Davis-Monthan AFB and flew Voodoos from March 1960 to December 1964. The 15th was inactivated on Christmas Eve 1964. (D. Nichols)

In March 1964, this 29th FIS Voodoo flying out of Malmstrom AFB still has no IR seeker and still has a natural-metal motif. (R. Robertson)

An open house at Westover AFB in 1966 has this 49th FIS from Griffiss AFB on display. The 49th had Voodoos from August 1959 to July 1968. (Ron Picciani)

This F-101B from the 59th FIS has the Falcon tail marking from the 322nd FIS. On 18 August 1968 the 322nd FIS at Kingsley Field, Oregon, was redesignated the 59th FIS to keep alive the heritage of ADC's more historical FISs. This Voodoo was sitting on the Eglin AFB ramp in Texas on 21 May 1969. (J. Morris)

A 62nd FIS F-101B from K. I. Sawyer AFB, Michigan, taxis on the Tyndall ramp in July 1968. In April 1971 the 62nd would lose its Voodoos to the Minnesota ANG, and inactivate on 30 April 1971. (J. Morris)

Showing remnants of 60th FIS markings, this 83rd FIS Voodoo, with a blue fuselage band, was photographed on 18 September 1960. This Voodoo would burn at Tyndall AFB on 22 May 1967. (Paul Stevens Collection)

In May 1968 these three Voodoos from the 84th FIS at Hamilton AFB bank away from the photo ship. On 30 September 1968, after flying Voodoos since April 1959, the 84th was inactivated but would "rise again from the ashes." (USAF)

A 98th FIS F-101F sits on the Nevada ANG ramp during the summer of 1966 during a cross-country training mission. She was a long way from home at Suffolk County AFB. This Voodoo was later destroyed in a mid-air collision on 12 December 1966. (Paul Stevens Collection)

On or about 1 June 1959, this natural-metal F-101B begins its taxi at Hamilton AFB. With just the 322nd FIS emblem on the tail, this Voodoo would be assigned at Kingsley Field, Oregon, from the 84th FIS. (USAF)

This 322nd FIS F-101B was transient at Travis AFB on 25 August 1968. On 30 September 1968 the 322nd was redesignated the 59th FIS at Kingsley Field and a 59th FIS emblem would replace the 322nd. (Pete Lewis)

The squadron commander's and a flight leader's Voodoos are from the 437th FIS at Oxnard AFB sitting on the Nellis AFB ramp on 7 October 1960. The golden yellow fuselage and tail markings were eye-catching. (Doug Olson)

Later tail markings of the 437th FIS were not as eye-catching, as can be seen on this 437th Voodoo on display at Mt. Home AFB, Idaho, in May 1967. The 437th flew Voodoos from October 1959 to April 1968. (Frank MacSorley)

An early 444th FIS F-101B on the ramp at Nellis AFB on 22 September 1962. This view of the natural-metal Voodoo was awesome to behold. The 444th flew the Voodoos out of Charleston AFB from March 1960 to July 1968. On 30 September 1968 the unit was inactivated. (Doug Olson)

Here is a 444th FIS Voodoo in August 1967; the "ADC Gray" paint looks good. (Via Harry Gann)

Four years later, the 445th FIS had these new tail markings. This 445th F-101F was on the Andrews AFB transient ramp on 9 September 1968. (Frank MacSorley)

The Air Defense Weapons Center (ADWC) at Tyndall AFB had eye-catching tail markings. This F-101B from the ADWC was on the Andrews AFB ramp on 26 August 1972. (Steve Miller)

During William Tell 1978, the 2nd Fighter Interceptor Training Squadron at Tyndall used the Voodoo at targets. This super shot of F-101B 57-0265 shows "fire in the hole" from the afterburner cans. Note, no IR seeker. Tyndall had 85 Voodoos assigned from 21 October 1958 to 21 September 1982 with 14 losses. (Ron Picciani)

Finally the ultimate version of the 1954 interceptor, the F-106 Delta Dart arrived to an ADC FIS when two F-106s were delivered to the 539th FIS at McGuire AFB on 30 May 1959. The 539th would become involved with the Category 3 testing until the spring of 1960. This involved weapons, SAGE, and aircraft compatibility. The 539th would not be the first to sit on alert; that "honor" would go to the 498th FIS at Geiger Field, Washington. This nice early picture of 539th F-106s in the fall of 1959 shows the 1st tail markings. Note that the 539th emblem was on both sides of the tail. (USAF/ Doug Barbier Collection)

The 539th FIS later on would adopt this lightning bolt tail marking around the 1966 time frame. Note the different star motifs in this 10 March 1967 picture on the Ft. Campbell, Kentucky, AAF ramp. The 539th, on 1 June 1967, would cease alert operations and inactivate on 31 August 1967. (Bill Malerba)

On 1 July 1971, the 2nd FIS was activated in ADC for the second time at Wurtsmith AFB with F-106s and personnel from the 94th FIS. On 1 October 1972, the "Horney Horses" would cease alert. The Delta Darts would transfer to the 171st FIS, Michigan ANG at Selfridge. The 2nd FIS inactivated on 31 March 1973. These 2nd FIS F-106s were photographed on 25 July 1971 at Patrick AFB. (Bill Strandberg)

The 5th FIS CO Lt. Colonel D. J. Parson's 106 sits on the Andrews AFB ramp in January 1971. This "Six" would crash on 8 May 1974. (Frank MacSorley)

Two F-106s from the 5th FIS alert detachment at Davis-Monthan AFB join up on a T-33 at 39,000 feet, east of Tucson. Getting a T-bird to this altitude has to be some sort of record but the winter weather had clouds down to the tops of the mountains. Photograph taken in January 1978. The 5th FIS and its 106s would be transferred to TAC on 1 October. (Doug Barbier)

On 23 June 1960, the 11th FIS at Duluth MAP, Minnesota, received its first two F-106s. On 1 May 1965 Lt. Colonel Curtis Utterback took over the 11th and this picture shows his 106 two weeks later. This Six would crash on 28 May 1981 with the 87th FIS. (Doug Remington)

An 11th FIS F-106A taxis in from a mission in July 1968. On 30 September 1968 the 11th would be redesignated the 87th FIS. (Jack Morris)

The early F-102 230-gallon external fuel tanks were used on F-106s. The tank was integral with the pylon but the weak retaining bolt design led to many tanks falling off the aircraft by accident. This frequently happened when the afterburner lit on takeoff. In one better forgotten incident, an 11th FIS Six buzzed the neighboring BOMARC launch site while returning from a NORAD night exercise at o'dark thirty early in the morning—a bored Lieutenant who got the "last scramble" decided to buzz the BOMARC facility while returning from the mission around 2:00 am. As he reached the perime-ter, he plugged in the afterburner and pulled the jet to the vertical and disappeared into the night.

While landing a few minutes later, he noticed all sorts of flashing red lights and heightened activity over at the BOMARC site. What had happened became clear when he shut down the jet in the barn—he was missing one of the external fuel tanks. He'd made a perfect LABS "toss bomb" delivery on the BOMARC site. A couple of cases of beer got the crew chief to download the other tank before dawn and pretend that the whole event never happened. Ah, the good old days.

A 48th FIS Six on display at Andrews AFB in May 1961. Note the large squadron emblem. This early tail marking was on both sides. Later this large emblem was also applied to the early white tail band. The 48th received its first F-106 on 15 September 1960 at Langley AFB. Note the 230-gallon F-102 wing tank. (Via Norm Taylor)

A 27th FIS F-106A, 59-0023, begins takeoff roll at Loring AFB, Maine, in this July 1967 photograph. The 27th received its first F-106 on 16 October. The 27th FIS was reactivated to replace the 27th. (Jim Sandvik)

On 16 May 1970 the 48th FIS had this Six on display at Langley. (Doug Remington)

In early 1976 the 48th started to apply this blue-and-white scheme to its Sixes—new markings for the Bicentennial. (J. Rotramel)

June 1976 sees the 48th conducting tanker operations. On 1 October 1979 the 48th FIS and its 106s at Langley would be transferred to TAC. (USAF)

On 30 September 1968 the 438th FIS at Griffiss AFB is redesignated the 49th FIS. This picture shows 59-0021 in early 49th markings in May 1969 at Otis AFB. (J. Winterbottom)

59-0021 was shot at Andrews AFB on 3 March 1973. This Six has the markings of the 21st Air Division CO, Maj. General James D. Price. The 106 would be struck by lightning on 15 May 1973, crashing and killing General Price. (Jack Morris)

The Bicentennial 106 of the 49th FIS, 59-0076, was on the New Jersey ANG ramp in April 1976. (Ted Woodo)

By July 1976, 59-0076 sported new tail markings in red. On 1 October 1979 the 49th FIS and its 106s would transfer to TAC. (Doug Remington)

The 71st FIS at Selfridge AFB received its first F-106A on 17 October 1960 and by 31 December eight are assigned to the squadron. This picture was taken later in May 1970 while based at Malmstrom AFB. On 1 July 1971 the 71st FIS transferred to TAC; personnel and 106s to the 319th at Malmstrom AFB. (Doug Miller)

Effective on 30 September 1968, the 498th FIS relocated to Hamilton AFB from Paine Field and was redesignated the 84th FIS. This nicely marked 84th 106 was on the Eglin AFB ramp in July 1971. (Tom Brewer)

In the 1974/1975 time frame, ADC tail markings were reduced in scope because General Royal Baker, ADC Vice Commander, came to the conclusion that less paint would save ADC money. I guess Lt. Gen. Baker forgot how his F-86 Sabre was painted in Korea. The 84th had this marking in November 1974. (George Bracken)

The 84th FIS is now back to full markings, this Six is leaving Peterson Field in February 1979. (Marty Isham)

Shortly after being redesignated the 87th FIS on 30 September 1968, this ex-11th FIS 106 has the 87th emblem on the tail. (Barbier Collection)

In August 1976, Squadron CO Lt. Colonel John Perkins' F-106 sits for her portrait. (Don Logan)

F-106B, 57-2539, from the 94th FIS, sits on the Selfridge AFB ramp in this August 1960 shot. (R. Volker)

On 30 April 1960, F-106A, 58-0796, arrived to the 94th FIS, the first Six to arrive. Fate would not be kind to this aircraft. On 13 August 1961, 796 would be the first loss of the 94th. While landing, the left tire blew, sheared the gear, went off the runway, and had extensive fire damage. The pilot was okay. This accident photograph shows foam that was sprayed on the Six. (USAF)

Showing 94th FIS markings out of Wurtsmith AFB in January 1971, Captain Denton's Six sits under a cold rain on the McChord AFB ramp. On 1 July 1971, the 94th FIS was transferred to TAC and the F-106s and personnel went to the 2nd FIS. (Doug Remington)

Effective 1 July 1963, the 95th relocated to Dover AFB, Delaware. These Sixes show the later markings in June 1970 during a transient at Andrews AFB. Note the two different shades of blue. (Jack Morris)

During William Tell 1972, Mr. Bones showed up with new tail markings and finished last in the F-106 category. The 95th would not be around too much longer. On 1 November 1972, it ceased alert operations and inactivated on 31 January 1973. Its Sixes went to the 119th FIS, New Jersey ANG. (Frank MacSorley)

This 318th FIS F-106A from McChord AFB is over the rugged but picturesque Northwest. On the tail is the original North Star marking with the 325th Fighter Wing in the center. (USAF)

The 318th FIS at McChord AFB received its first F-106 on 21 March 1960 and has the "official" arrival on 24 March 1960 when two F-106s arrive. This May 1965 shot shows the original North Star tail marking. (H. Rued)

By July 1968, the 318th FIS was showing this tail marking. (Pete Lewis)

The 318th had F-106A, 58-0776, in a special Bicentennial Freedom Bird paint scheme for the 1976 festivities. This Six would crash on 29 August 1979. (Doug Remington)

Close-up of 58-0776 nose gear door and canopy area. (Doug Remington)

During Red Flag 78-05, F-106A, 59-0054, of the 318th bumped an A-7D of the 76th TFS on 25 July 1978. The Six lost her nose but landed at Michael Army Air Field at Dugway, Utah. The A-7 crashed but the pilot ejected safely. (Doug Barbier)

Close-up of 59-0054 nose area. This Six was repaired and flown again with the 318th in the fall of 1979. (Doug Barbier)

A 318th FIS F-106A on the ramp at Peterson AFB, Colorado, on 3 June 1978. The "new" North Star tail marking was eye-catching. On 1 October 1979 the 318th and its F-106s were transferred to TAC. (M. Isham)

On 2 February 1960 the 319th at Bunker Hill AFB, Indiana, received its first two Sixes. This shot was taken in 1962. On 6 February 1963, F-106s begin to leave the 319th with the impending move to Homestead AFB to fly F-104s. The last F-106 to leave Bunker Hill AFB was on 9 March. (W. Gatschet)

The 319th FIS is reactivated in ADC on 1 July 1971 to replace the 71st FIS at Malmstrom AFB. The 319th has all the ex-Sixes and personnel from the 71st FIS. The 319th stands down from alert on 1 April 1972 and is inactivated on 30 April 1972. (Doug Remington)

Showing its early tail markings, this 329th FIS F-106A from George AFB is on display at Hill AFB, Utah, in May 1962. On 29 July 1960 the 329th received its first two F-106s. This F-106A, 59-0118, would crash on 11 June 1966. On 1 May 1967, the 329th ceased alert activities and inactivated on 31 July 1967. The last two Sixes flew out on 9 June 1967. (J. Fitzgibbons)

Kincheloe AFB, Michigan, and the 438th FIS received its first F-106 on 12 May 1960. This picture shows F-106A, 59-0076, in July 1968. On 30 September 1968 the 438th at Griffiss AFB is redesignated the 49th FIS. By the end of August 1968, the 438th began the move to Griffiss. (B. Strandberg)

On 16 September 1959, F-106A, 58-0761, arrives to the 456th FIS at Castle AFB, California. This shot has 57-2482 on display in May 1968 before relocating to Oxnard AFB, effective on 2 July 1968. On 18 July 1968, the 456th FIS is redesignated the 437th FIS. (R. Lawson Collection)

Because there isn't an exact date of this photo, these two F-106s could be from the 437th FIS. The 437th didn't have the Six for long, for in another HQ ADC "shuffle," the 437th is redesignated the 460th FIS on 30 September 1967. (D. Barbier Collection)

Still with ex-437th FIS tail colors, this 460th FIS is on the Tyndall AFB ramp in February 1970 after relocating to Kingsley Field on 1 December 1969 from Oxnard AFB. (Tom Brewer)

In March 1971, HQ ADC informs the 460th FIS that it will relocate from Kingsley Field to Grand Forks AFB, North Dakota. The move was completed on 30 June 1971. This 460th F-106A with new markings was photographed in April 1973 at Wright-Patterson AFB. This Six crashed on 18 July 1979 with the 194th FIS, California ANG. On 1 May 1974, the 460th FIS ceased alert operations, and on 15 July 1974 inactivated with its F-106s transferred to the 194th FIS. (Tom Brewer)

The 498th FIS would relocate to McChord AFB on 1 July 1963 from Spokane IAP, Washingon, (Geiger Field). This 498th Six with the early North Star tail marking was photographed in late May 1966. (Frank MacSorley)

Another move on 15 June 1966 has the 498th deploying to Paine Field. While at Paine, tail markings designed by Colonel James D. Price were applied. This photo in August 1968 at Paine Field shows that impressive tail scheme. On 30 September 1968, the 498th relocates once again, to Hamilton AFB and is redesignated the 84th FIS. On or about 15 September, the 498th had been relieved of alert duties and had begun moving to Hamilton AFB. (Frank MacSorley)

An ADWC F-106B in markings of the Commander of ADC, Lt. General Thomas K. McGehee, flies over the new Panama City, Florida, marina. This F-106 would crash shortly after takeoff on 30 September 1971 with the loss of the two pilots onboard. Note that the ADC eagle on the tail faces forward on this side of the airplane. (USAF)

It's now May 1969 and Brig. General James D. Price is CO of the Air Defense Weapons Center at Tyndall AFB. This beautiful air-to-air photo shows Price in 59-0004, El Jefe, flying with CINC ADC General Agan's F-106B, getting some "Texas Gas." 59-0004 would later crash with the 318th FIS on 24 June 1980. (USAF)

ack when Colonel Price was CO of the 498th FIS at Geiger Field, he designed the 498th FIS tail markings, which became the 84th FIS tail marking. When now-Brig. General Price took over the ADWC, he picked up the phone and asked the CO of the 84th FIS if he could have the 84th markings for the ADWC. Needless to say, the 84th CO stood firm and said, "No." So General Price had to design a new red, white, and blue scheme for the ADWC, hence F-106A 59-0004, *El Jefe* and the rest of the Tyndall aircraft.

An F-106 assigned to the ADWC at Tyndall AFB carries a modified AIM-26B during a (Simple High Accuracy Guidance) SHAG test mission over the Gulf of Mexico. (USAF photo Barbier Collection)

While commander of NORAD/ADCOM, General "Chappie" James had F-106B, 59-0165, from the ADWC as his personal aircraft. Here is his Six on the Peterson AFB ramp on 4 December 1977. General James retired on 6 December 1977 and his Six would burn at Tyndall on 27 February 1980. (Marty Isham)

During William Tell 1978, the ADWC commander's F-106A, belonging to Brig. General Wainwright, returns from a mission. Note that the CO's stripes continue under the belly of the Six. (Ron Picciani)

Chapter Five

F-4E, 66-345, 57th FIS, Keflavik, Iceland, flies formation with a T-33. This photo shows the "Lance" design that was carried on the external fuel tanks until the summer of 1979. The ADC badge is prominently displayed on the right intake trunk. Photo was taken March 1979. The 57th FIS and its F-4Es would transfer to TAC on 1 October 1979. (D. Barbier)

Icelandic Operations

F-102 Delta Dagger, F-4C Phantom II

During the height of the Cold War in the 1950s and 1960s, there was no more strategic piece of real estate for basing USAF Interceptors patrolling the North Atlantic than the country of Iceland. Round-the-clock intercepts of Soviet Tu-95 Bear bombers traversing that ocean were flown by the Air Defense Command.

After the end of World War II, when the Cold War began to get warm, the nation of Iceland joined NATO in 1949. But there was a catch…Iceland didn't have to have its own armed forces, and no foreign forces would be stationed there during peacetime. The Icelandic government would soon change its mind because of the Berlin Crisis and the Korean Invasion. In May 1951, the United States and Iceland signed a treaty stating that the United States would defend Iceland and the surrounding waters. But, a year later in summer 1952, the USAF still hadn't arrived, and the Icelandic government informed the United States that the USAF aircraft promised for its air defense had to be on the ramp by 1 September or the United States was no longer welcome in Iceland. After departing George AFB on 26 August 1952, the 192nd Fighter Bomber Squadron, Nevada ANG (activated for the Korean War), arrived at Keflavik Airport on 1 September 1952 and eight F-51D Mustangs are shown sitting on alert. A total of 24 Mustangs would be assigned. This photo shows the 192nd Mustangs shortly after their arrival. On 1 December 1952, the 496th fighter bomber squadron (FBS) was activated to replace the 192nd, which returned to stateside control. (USAF)

In October 1952, HQ USAF informed HQ ADC that the 82nd FIS at Larson AFB would be moving to Iceland in the spring of 1953. The new all-weather interceptor was needed for the nasty Icelandic weather to replace the Mustangs. During the first week of March 1953, the 82nd began the move to Keflavik Airport. Effective 1 April 1953, the 82nd FIS, with its F-94Bs, were assigned to MATS from ADC at Keflavik. This F-94B from the 82nd, FA-816 Jan IV, shares the ramp with Sabres enroute to USAFE. The diagonal nose band was red with white trim. It appears that the forward section of the tip tank has just been replaced. (B. Sveinsson Collection)

This somewhat faded, but extremely rare and historic photo provides a proper sense of history. Crews of the 82nd FIS race for their F-94Bs during the summer of 1954 while practicing yet another scramble. Note that the 82nd markings are now more eye-catching and the 82nd emblem is on the aircraft. On 9 October 1954, the 82nd F-94Bs would begin to leave Iceland. (USAF via Dana Bell)

On 10 November 1954, the first 57th F-89C lands at Keflavik Airport from Presque Isle AFB, and on 12 November the unit is assigned to the Iceland Air Defense Force (MATS) from ADC. This 57th F-89C flies over the rugged and snowy Icelandic landscape in spring 1955. (Authors' Collection)

In November 1955, the first three F-89Ds arrived to the 57th FIS. The F-89Cs were flown out to depot and the ANG. This undated F-89D photo of the 57th shows a bit of wear on its rocket pod. Note the absence of underwing auxiliary fuel tanks. (USAF via D. Barbier)

Effective on 1 July 1962, the 57th FIS and Icelandic Air Defense are now under ADC. On 5 July 1962, the first F-102s arrive and on 20 September 1962, the Deuces have replaced the Scorpions in the alert barns. This F-102A photo shows small, dark-blue checks on the rudder in March 1965 on the Keflavik ramp. Note no IR on the nose. (Tom Brewer)

Concerning those small checks on the rudder, it's now summer 1966 and the dark-blue checks have been replaced with light-blue ones; the tail and wingtips are now a fluorescent red instead of arctic red (insignia red). (Pete Bracci)

Around 1969, the 57th FIS began to put the larger black-and-white checkerboard pattern on the rudder. This 1970 Bear D intercept shows these larger checks. (USAF)

The first F-4Cs arrived at Keflavik on 16 April 1973 and replaced the Deuces in the alert barn on 1 July 1973. On 3 July 1973, this Phantom II, 63-7475, flew the first Bear intercept mission. (USAF via Bob Roder)

Newly arrived F-4C, 63-7412, sits on the 57th FIS squadron ramp at Keflavik, Iceland, while an F-102 prepares to return to the United States and be placed in the boneyard at Davis-Monthan AFB. On 17 July 1973, the last three F-102s would leave Iceland. The 57th FIS was the last Deuce FIS in ADC. (USAF via D. Barbier)

Bicentennial marked 57th FIS F-4C taking the arresting cable at Keflavik, Iceland. Note the open air-refueling door, which depressurizes the external fuel tanks. (D. Barbier Collection)

The 57th FIS took its F-4Cs to William Tell 1976 at Tyndall and captured third place in the F-4 category. The weapons meet ran from 31 October to 21 November 1976. The 57th, with its F-4Cs, competed against three F-4E teams. Here F-4C, 63-7529, pauses on her taxi-in for the meet. Note the PQM-102s in the background. (R. Leader)

On 4 May 1978, 57th FIS F-4E, 66-328, touches down on the runway at Keflavik, Iceland, after a practice intercept mission. When the F-4Es first arrived on 21 March 1978, they were in the standard Southeast Asia jungle camouflage. Both 328 and 334 then had the black-and-white checkerboard applied over the standard camo. As these aircraft cycled through the depot at Getafe, Spain, they were repainted with the lower-visibility overall gloss "ADC Gray." (Baldur Sveinsson/Barbier Collection)

F-4E, 66-0300, begins to bank away from the camera in this June 1979 photograph, offering a really nice angle to view McDonnell's twin-engine fighter. (D. Barbier)

57th FIS T-33A, 58-0575, cruises over solid undercast in this June 1979 photo. The pilot's name is on the front canopy rail, while the crew chief's is on the rear. Checks on the tails were hand painted and each aircraft was slightly different. Note the high-visibility orange markings—not red. (D. Barbier)

Trailing a typical smoky exhaust trail behind it, an F-4E from the 57th FIS closes in on two T-33s while completing a practice intercept off the southern coast of Iceland during June 1979. When the original engines were installed, it was possible to visually acquire an F-4 at ranges in excess of 50 miles if the lighting conditions were just right. (D. Barbier)

This one-of-a-kind photograph shows a Bear Foxtrot cruising southbound between Iceland and Greenland at 23,000 feet in July 1979. This photograph was taken from a T-33 and this was the only time a T-33 ever successfully intercepted one of the Soviet bombers. The T-33 had been paired on the intercept by the Rockville, Iceland, ground control intercept (GCI) unit while the T-33 was in the traffic pattern at Keflavik Airport. (D. Barbier)

T-33A, 58-0540, Jaws painted in camouflage with a special training AIM-9 missile unit underwing that could track an aerial target and indicate an electronic "kill" to a ground station while the aircraft's pilot was performing Air Combat Maneuvering (ACM). That information could then be used for playback of actual gun camera footage from the mission during the debrief. (D. Barbier Collection)

A 57th FIS F-4E with a Bear, exact date unknown. (USAF)

Up-close and personal with a Bear, exact date unknown. (USAF)

Remember the 57th FIS F-4Cs? Seven of them arrived at the ADWC at Tyndall AFB in April/May 1978 to replace seven other F-4Cs that had arrived from TAC in 1977. Major Rich Maki had flown in the first F-4C at Tyndall on 15 June 1977 from Luke AFB. This shot shows 63-7475, an ex-57th F-4C, on the Tyndall ramp on 4 October 1978, still wearing its Vietnam camouflage paint scheme. (M. Isham)

A nice taxi shot of F-4C 63-7589 in "ADC Gray" during William Tell 1978. Note the MiG kill red star below front cockpit. This Phantom was also an ex-57th FIS aircraft. (R. Leader)

While the 57th converted to F-4Es, its personnel had to go to school in the Continental United States (CONUS). While in school, the 87th deployed to Iceland to stand alert for the 57th. From on or about 20 April 1978 to 13 May 1978, eight F-106s were on the 57th's ramp. This tail shot of 59-0091 seems to say it all about the TDY. (Baldur Sveinsson)

F-106A, 59-0091, would fly an intercept with Captain Bill Thomas. Three active scrambles were accomplished, one night and two daylight intercepts of which one was in really nasty instrument conditions weather. (D. Barbier)

Chapter Six

In July 1969, the 30th Air Division Headquarters had this pristine North American T-39A Sabreliner assigned for various VIP travel assignments. (A. Swanberg)

Support Aircraft

T-33 Shooting Star, C-54 Skymaster,
C-119 Flying Boxcar, EC-121 Warning Star, B-57 Canberra

It has been said in Air Force circles that "Fighters make movies" but "Bombers make history." We can proudly add one more phrase to this collection: "Support aircraft make squadrons." Without these cargo, liaison, radar patrol, and VIP transport aircraft, there would be no trophy-winning squadrons of sleek jet interceptors.

The "Ultimate Hack," a VB-17G on the Boeing ramp on 30 July 1956. This sparkling Flying Fortress belonged to the 8th Air Division CO at McClellan AFB, California, that commanded the 551st and 552nd AEW&C Wings. Note the curtains in the waist gunner's window. This B-17 appeared in the movie "The Lady Takes a Flyer" in 1958 with an ugly green and brown paint job. (Via A. Lloyd)

Headquartered at Selfridge AFB, the 4708th Air Defense Wing flew this North American B-25J in the 1950s. (D. Barbier Collection)

A 328th Combat Support Group Douglas C-47A Skytrain from Richards-Gebaur AFB, Missouri, sits on the Sioux City Airport ramp on 27 July 1965. Originally delivered to the Army Air Forces as a troop transport in World War II, the legendary C-47 was an airplane that just couldn't be replaced, serving proudly with the USAF into the early-1970s. (N. Taylor Collection)

This Douglas C-54D Skymaster from HQ ADC sits at Peterson Field in the late-1950s. The windows suggest a VIP aircraft, perhaps from the far north. (R. McCarthy)

Douglas C-118A from the 4650th Combat Support Squadron, "Dog Patch Airlines," sits on the Richards-Gebaur ramp on 4 July 1971. This C-118A is actually an ex-U.S. Navy R6D-1, 131596. (N. Taylor Collection)

A Fairchild C-119F, also from the 4650th Combat Support Squadron, has suffered some engine problems at Missoula, Montana, on 19 November 1968. (A. Swanberg)

Hamilton AFB was home to Det 2, 4650th Combat Support Squadron. Here is a Det 2 Fairchild C-123B Provider on the Hamilton ramp on 21 May 1966. (W. T. Larkins)

With the impressive Pike's Peak as a backdrop, this Convair T-29C from the 4600th Air Base Wing at Peterson Field taxies in from a navigational training mission in 1967. (USAF)

This classic Cessna U-3A Blue Canoe (military version of the civilian model 310B) sports an ADC emblem while posing on the ramp in the mid-1960s. (Editor's Note: We can't run this photo and not mention that this airplane is the Air Force's version of Sky King's famed TV steed, the Songbird!) (J. Geer)

The 17th Tow Target Squadron at Vincent AFB received its Martin B-57 Canberras in July 1956, equipped to tow the "rag" for aerial gunnery target training. This is a photo of airborne BA-289 soon after arrival. (USAF)

B-57E, 55-4273, arrived to the 4713th Defense Systems Evaluation Squadron on 17 October 1961 at Stewart AFB. During a training flight on 23 August 1962, the fire-warning light came on. While making a precautionary landing at Duluth International Airport, the B-57 hit a hill short of the runway and skidded to a stop on the runway. As seen in this picture, a salvageable aircraft still sits on the ground. Note the foam on the runway. (USAF)

B-57E, 55-4273, was full of surprises that fateful day. After having come to rest at the end of its crash landing, the Duluth Airport firefighters did a masterful job ensuring there would be no risk of fire by expending every ounce of foam available in their crash trucks. During the recovery process, however, a spark from an electrical connection suddenly ignited fuel vapors, triggering a massive aircraft fire. (USAF)

Believe it or not, ADC did have North American F-100 Super Sabres assigned. They were at the 4758th DSES at Biggs AFB, Texas. Fourteen F-100Cs and one two-seat F-100F were assigned and used in support of the Army's Air Defense Missile Training at Fort Bliss from July 1962 to August 1970. The 4758th suffered only two F-100C losses in 1963, on 13 May and 22 November. (USAF)

In November 1962, Major James Fitzgibbon was able to photograph his RB-57D-11 at Hill AFB. The 4677th defense systems evaluation squadron (DSES) flew the long-wing B-57s from 1959 to 1964 as high-altitude targets. Wing-spar fractures led to the airplanes' retirement from ADC. (J. Fitzgibbon)

To extend the radar coverage offshore, Lockheed RC-121 Warning Stars were used to support the ADC fighter squadrons. In 1958, as a 552nd AEW&C Wing, RC-121D is heading out over the Pacific on patrol. She is buzzed by two 83rd FIS Lockheed F-104As. (USAF)

For patrolling the Atlantic, the 551st AEW&C Wing flew Radar Connies from Otis AFB. This RC-121D was photographed at MacArthur Airport on Long Island, New York, on 7 September 1963 as it arrived for static display at the annual Columbus Day Weekend Airshow. (Jim Hawkins)

In the 1950s, the 85th FIS at Scott AFB had one of the better color schemes on its T-33s. Note the gun port. (D. Slowiak Collection)

The 328th Fighter Wing out of Richards-Gebaur AFB used T-33s for support and proficiency missions. Note the 328th Fighter Wing travel pod. (D. Slowiak Collection)

The Commander's T-33A of the Sioux City Air Defense Sector suffers through a bit of rain. (D. Slowiak Collection)

A 1st Fighter Wing Air Defense T-33A sits on the Selfridge AFB ramp. (D. Slowiak Collection)

As we know, ADC had to keep its operational forces in tip-top shape around the clock. So when an engine, engine parts, or a piece of aircraft was needed, something had to be done logistically. In the early years, each squadron had its own cargo-type aircraft. For example, the 14th Fighter Group, 37th FIS, had a Fairchild C-119. Also, Air Force Logistics Command (AFLC) contracted-out for parts delivery from maintenance depots. But, as we know, sometimes people and parts had to be delivered "yesterday!"

On 1 September 1959, HQ ADC activated the 4650th Combat Support Squadron at Richards-Gebaur AFB. This was to streamline "trash hauling" operations in ADC. With the headquarters at Richards-Gebaur, Det 1 was activated at Stewart AFB, New York, and Det 2 was activated at Hamilton AFB. The 4650th soon acquired the nickname "Dogpatch Airlines" because it could haul anything, anywhere, any time. The squadron began flying Douglas C-54s and Fairchild C-123s in September 1959. By December 1969, it had completed 10 years of accident-free flying, even with a conversion to C-119s from C-123s in 1967. By 1969, the C-54s had been replaced by larger pressurized C-118s. By 1 January 1969, Dogpatch Airlines had six C-118s at Richards-Gebaur, nine C-119s at Stewart, and nine C-119s at Hamilton.

The unit was deactivated on 31 July 1972, and with the demise of "Dog Patch Airlines," needed parts wound up being strapped in the back seats of T-33s.

This 30th Air Division-marked T-Bird was one of the more eye-catching paint jobs in 1964. (D. Slowiak Collection)

Chapter Seven

YF-12, 06934, was the only Blackbird to wear an ADC emblem. It was damaged beyond repair by fire at Edwards after a landing accident on 14 August 1966; its rear half was salvaged and mated with the front half of a Lockheed static test airframe to create the one-and-only SR-71C. That aircraft was nicknamed "The Bastard" by its pilots, as it did not fly quite straight and true. It was unique among all SR-71s; it carried the ventral fins under its nacelles—a leftover of its YF-12 lineage, which did not exist on any other SR-71. (T. Landis Collection)

What Might Have Been

F-106X, YF-12 Blackbird, NAA Retaliator, USAF F-14 Tomcat

While you've seen all the different aircraft utilized to best advantage by the Air Defense Command, you can only dream of what might have been had military egos, corporate politics, and advanced aviation technology somehow been different. What would've happened had the Air Force purchased Mach 3 YF-12s?

In March 1958, before the first two F-106s arrived at the 539th FIS, Convair San Diego proposed an F-106-30 Interceptor Weapons System. This proposal was the culmination of the previous 10 years of development of the F-102/F-106 aircraft. The two-man F-106-30 was to be the primary defense against all air-breathing threats that would be encountered from the mid 1960s to the early 1970s. The redesigned -30 airframe would have a canard control surface, internal compression inlets, and a bi-convex, variable-camber wing. The fuselage would have been wrapped around a Pratt & Whitney J-58 proposed engine with 30,600-pound static sea level thrust, which would give the -30 Delta Dart a Mach 2.5 design speed. Armament carried would have been the GAR-9 (GAR-X) semi-active HE/nuclear warhead missiles. The GAR-9 (Hughes AIM-47A) armament would have been capable of carrying out zoom attacks to 88,000 feet with kill capability to 100,000 feet. This photo shows an early F-106-30 proposal model. (Isham Collection)

In October 1967, from another updated Convair proposal, the Office of the Secretary of Defense (OSD) recommended that an improved F-106 called the F-106X replace the F-12. The F-106X would have look-down and shoot-down targeting capability, and the potential cost of four F-106Xs would have equaled just one F-12. This is a photo of the F-106X proposal. (Isham Collection)

This factory concept model shows the F-14B's armament/fuel-tank layout. Grumman offered the F-14B for the Air Force IMI in the summer of 1972 and had its first flight on 12 September 1973. In April 1974 the F-14B proposal officially died, as would ADCOM itself in 1979. (Isham Collection)

Enter the Grumman F-14 Tomcat. On 12 June 1969, in testimony before the House Appropriations Committee, Assistant Secretary of the Air Force for Research and Development G. L. Hansen testifies: "Candidates for this role [a modern air defense interceptor] included the F-106X, F-12, F-14 [a proposed Navy aircraft], or some possible new interceptor." On 21 December 1970, the F-14 first flew at Grumman's Calverton test facility on eastern Long Island, New York. In summer 1972, this impressive and highly believable full-scale mock-up of the F-14 Air Force IMI was rolled out in full ADCOM markings. (R. Sherry Collection)

The pages of aviation history are filled with stories about what might have happened had certain airplanes been in the Air Force inventory at certain times. In the case of the Grumman F-14 Tomcat and McDonnell Douglas F-15 Eagle, the history of the Air Defense Command would have been dramatically rewritten if they had these airplanes in the time of actual war. Compared to the earlier-generation F-104 and F-106, these two 1970s-era aircraft possessed performance levels and weapon payload capability that was simply undreamed of in the 1960s.

8 April 1974—Lt. General "Chappie" James (Deputy Assistant Sec Def [PA]) flew in an F-14 at NAS Miramar as the Radar Operator. "...so it's in being and it's a helluva weapons system."

1 September 1975—General "Chappie" James is CINC ADCOM/NORAD. He and his staff are looking at all Improved Manned Interceptor (IMI) proposals. The F-106 needs a replacement, and fast.

29 September 1975—HQ USAF advised ADCOM that the F-15 selection as the follow-on interceptor (FOI) would be supported in the FY78 program objectives memorandum (POM).

5 May 1976—The F-15 was identified as the FOI. Six F-106 squadrons are proposed to receive the F-15 in FY80. The F-106s are to go to the ANG.

10 September 1976—The HQ USAF Studies and Analysis, at the direction of the Deputy Secretary of Defense, completed an Interceptor Comparison Study. The study did a complete re-evaluation of the F-14, F-15, and F-16 aircraft. The F-15 emerged as the best FOI. On 29 November 1976, General David C. Jones CSAF and Mr. Thomas Reed briefed the Deputy Secretary of Defense on the need for an FOI. The Deputy Secretary of Defense deferred selection of the FOI to the new administration, President Carter.

Fall 1977—The USAF/ADCOM are still looking for the FOI/IMI. Grumman still has a proposal with the F-14 but General James is told: "The USAF is not going to buy another Navy airframe!" This slams the lid on the F-14 IMI proposals.

6 December 1977—General James retires and is replaced by General James E. Hill.

2 June 1978—Two F-15As of the 49th TFW (TAC) at Holloman AFB, New Mexico, are standing ADCOM/NORAD alert.

EDITOR'S NOTE: The story of the Navy's F-14 versus the Air Force's F-15 is an interesting piece of military aviation history. Both represented quantum leaps in technology and featured airframe and powerplant improvements resulting from lessons learned in Southeast Asia, where U.S. fighters were lost at higher ratios than during the Korean War. New design features were identified to maintain air superiority, such as a 360-degree bubble canopy, smokeless engines, advanced flight control systems, and engines separated from one another for enhanced survivability.

While Grumman's successful bid to build the F-14 resulted in part from the company's experience with variable-geometry wing design and its work on the F-111B program, selecting a contractor to build the Air Force's next-generation air superiority fighter was a different matter. That selection came down to competing designs from McDonnell Douglas, North American, and Republic. All three proposals sported similar features and performance, but on 1 January 1970, McDonnell Douglas was announced as the winning contractor with its single-seat, twin-engine, twin-tail Eagle.

This decision spelled the end-of-the-line for fighter production at both North American and Republic, companies that had been in the fighter business since World War II. One of the factors working against Republic was that Grumman had just been awarded the F-14 contract, and there was no way America's two largest jet fighter programs would be built in New York within ten miles of each other. Republic then became a sub-contractor building components for other aircraft, including vertical stabilizers and aft fuselage sections for a new Navy fighter–the Grumman F-14 Tomcat!

Variations of operational Lockheed and North American aircraft were proposed as advanced interceptors for ADC, but neither came to pass.

On 7 August 1963, the first flight of the YF-12 with Lockheed test pilot Jim Eastham at the controls took place at the Groom Lake test facility. In March 1965, President Johnson

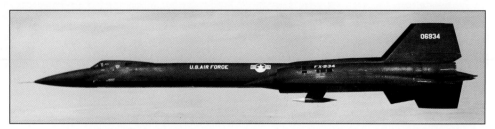

and Secretary of Defense McNamara said publicly that the F-12 was the interceptor sought by the Air Force. This is YF-12A, 06934, on 30 September 1964 over Edwards' Rogers Dry Lake area. (Isham Collection)

Another view of the ADC Blackbird. By 31 December 1967, the F-12 had been pronounced dead by the OSD and the F-106X proposal was substituted for it. (T. Landis Collection)

By 1971, ADC's Improved Manned Interceptor (IMI) had not been fulfilled. An F-106 replacement was still not on any ADC Squadron ramp. Plans were being made for the ANG to get the F-106 in 1972. This is North American's proposal for a three-engine Vigilante called the Retaliator. It would have three General Electric J79-GE-10 turbojets providing a total of 35,610 pounds of thrust to carry advanced Falcon armament along with a GE gun. This ADC version of the RA-5C was the NAA proposal NR-349. Rear view of the Retaliator shows the three-engine exhaust configuration. (Isham Collection)

"The Reason for Air Defense." *On 1 October 1979, Air Defense Command Fighter Interceptor Squadrons ceased to exist. This Soviet Tupolev Tu-95 Bear bomber was the reason for the interceptors then and—believe it or not—now as well. As this book was being written, the same reason that the Air Defense Command was originally formed is still out there.* (Marv Cox)